S   OPOLI AN UN'VERS!

WHY YOUR CORPORATE CULTURE CHANGE ISN'T WORKING – AND WHAT TO DO ABOUT IT

WHY YOUR CORPORATE CULTURE CHANGE ISN'T WORKING – AND WHAT TO DO ABOUT IT

❖

Michael Ward

Gower

All characters in this book are ficticious, and any resemblence to living persons is purely co-incidental.

Published by
Gower Publishing Limited
Gower House
Croft Road
Aldershot
Hampshire GU11 3HR
England

Gower
Old Post Road
Brookfield
Vermont 05036
USA

Michael Ward has asserted his right under the Copyright, Designers and Patents Act 1988 to be identified as the author of this work.

British Library Cataloguing in Publication Data
Ward, Michael
Why Your Corporate Culture isn't Working:
And What to Do About it
I. Title
303.4
ISBN 0-566-07434-6

Library of Congress Cataloging-in-Publication Data
Ward, Michael, 1952–
    Why your corporate culture change isn't working – and what to do about it / Michael Ward.
    p.   cm
ISBN 0-586-07434-8
1. Corporate culture.   2. Organizational change.   I. Title
HD58.7.W33 1994
658.4'063—dc20 93-48280 CIP

Typeset in 11 point Garamond Light by Poole Typesetting (Wessex) Ltd and printed in Great Britain at the University Press, Cambridge.

IN MEMORY OF MY MOTHER, NÉE BEATRICE THERESA COSTELLO, AND MY
FATHER, JOHN JOSEPH WARD

CONTENTS

FIGURES

TABLES

PREFACE

For several years it has been a cliché to remark upon the ever-increasing rate of change in the world. That such an observation is cliché makes it no less true. Nearly everyone is aware of forces for change surrounding us and impacting upon our lives. Often we perceive change as threatening; we're not sure what it will entail. Usually we have severe doubts about our ability to handle it.

Yet many changes in our lives are beneficial. Today we enjoy a duration and standard of living unimaginable to inhabitants of previous centuries. No omnipotent emperor of old had access to antibiotics, telephones or air travel. One simple example perhaps serves to illustrate the degree of difference between our forebears and ourselves. Many of us go abroad on holiday two or three times a year. Typically, this is as often as our parents went abroad in their entire lives.

Irrespective of whether change is good or bad, it is nearly always deeply unsettling. Because change is deeply unsettling and because it is now so prevalent, the management of change is one of the great themes of our time. Management in the 1990s is about the management of change.

Individuals face change; so do organizations. Organizations form the crucial interface between the micro (individual) and the macro (societal) levels of humanity. This is of immense importance. Virtually all of us belong to organizations, work and social. When organizations fail then we fail – at initially an individual level and ultimately a societal level. If our company fails, we're out of work. If enough companies fail in our city, then our city will become economically depressed.

It is because the fates of individuals and organizations are entwined that domino effects are easily produced. If a multinational closes a local site, hundreds of suppliers lose trade. Workers are thrown on welfare; demand for many other goods and services collapses. Finally the corner sweet shop goes out of business.

Through organizations, wealth is created and well-being is determined. Our quality of life, as employees and as consumers, is profoundly affected. Formerly organizations seemed immutable; we somehow felt that they would last for ever. Now, with experience of global recession, their existence seems much more fragile.

Today organizations are under many pressures – political, economic, environmental, social, legal. The list is potentially endless. Each of these pressures implies change. Each of these changes will be felt at both micro and macro levels. Some of these changes will have domino effects which will also be experienced at micro and macro levels. It is not for nothing that we live in a global village.

Many, if not most, organizations face radical change. Markets expand and contract, technology revolutionizes whole industries, companies merge, take over, go public, re-privatize.

The old notion of change as a one-off occurrence is fast being replaced by the concept of change as a way of life. This generates imperatives which detract and distract from day-to-day operations. Simply keeping the business going is becoming ever harder.

Everywhere we encounter the paraphernalia of organizational change – the endless sheaves of mission statements, consumer guarantees of quality, of undying service, etc. And yet it's claimed that more than 80 per cent of change programmes fail – for a wide variety of reasons. If true, this staggering statistic has enormous power adversely to affect us at both individual and societal levels. For if organizations truly are the membrane dividing micro and macro levels, then failure at an organizational level ultimately means both micro and macro failure.

It is for this reason that I have written this book. It seeks directly to confront organizational change. Specifically it addresses the wide variety of reasons underlying the failure of organizational change. Examining what goes wrong gives us the chance to learn how to do things right.

This book owes little to academic theory or research. Although I was academically well versed before I began to effect organizational change, I found, to my intense chagrin, that my academic knowledge base was usually irrelevant. I was forced to devise my own concepts, hypotheses and theories, and then discover whether they worked in practice. What worked I kept; the rest were discarded.

Worse still, I found to my horror that many of those whom I encountered busily working to bring about organizational change travelled with frighteningly little intellectual luggage. Organizational change means dramatic change in the lives of many people – suppliers, employees, owners, consumers, people at all levels of society. Often the effects of change upon such lives are hard to predict, but terrible prices are paid. Thus, merrily to incite organizational change without relevant professional expertise is both extremely unprofessional and morally abhorrent.

This book aims to redress the imbalance caused by irrelevant theory and downright contempt of theory. Lessons are derived from what doesn't work – and what does.

Organizational change, particularly culture change, is not susceptible to an off-the-cuff set of instructions. General lessons are, emphatically, not procedures to be applied willy-nilly. Understanding of the problems of change is no substitute for professional help. Managers contemplating organizational change would do well to seek such help. DIY culture change makes about as much sense as DIY brain surgery.

By the end of this book, the reader should have a keen appreciation of which paths to follow – and which to avoid. The time and effort spent reading the book will save immensely more time and effort. Every time a change initiative fails, people suffer; next time around, change becomes even harder to attain. If it helps to cut some of this waste, my book will have served a worthy purpose.

The format I have chosen is deliberately simple. Part 1, Organizational Culture and Change, draws from practical examples precise and thereby highly useful definitions of culture and change. It develops some basic intellectual luggage to make some journeys through change.

Many people – and most managers – learn best from experience. The case studies in Parts II and III are vicarious experience of journeys through change. Part II, The Methodology of Change, deals with organizations moving towards culture change. Often the most damaging mistakes are made before such projects are properly under way. Ironically mistakes, which often come with horrific price tags, can easily be precluded. It just takes more time, more attention, more care and some professional help.

Part III, Implementing Change, deals with the most common errors experienced during such implementation. As with Part II, these errors will be all too recognizable to those who have made them.

Each case study consists of a narrative, followed by a discussion of relevant issues, key points raised and a concluding principle.

Part IV, Successful Culture Change, draws the material of the preceding parts together to develop best theory and practice.

Let's go !

Michael Ward

PART I

ORGANIZATIONAL CULTURE AND CHANGE

❖

AN EXAMPLE OF CULTURE

Thor Freyer, of the Trolltind company, was looking forward to his first meeting with Fernando Arocena of the Ibanez Corporation. Fernando, for his part, was excited. Both men had international reputations in biotechnology; each was, professionally speaking, well known to the other. Trolltind was market leader in Norway; Ibanez enjoyed similar status in Spain. Months of delicate, tentative overtures had resulted in a mooted joint venture which might, just might, lead towards common European dominance. Now Fernando and Thor were to conduct somewhat tougher negotiations – a necessary next step in their companies' courtship ritual. The venue chosen was the small, historic and beautiful English town of Chester. For Trolltind and Ibanez, it had two crucial advantages: it was discreet and it was neutral.

Unfortunately for both individuals and companies, Thor and Fernando quickly found that they simply couldn't work effectively together. Thor was discomfited by Fernando's habit of standing close to him and gesticulating excitedly. Each time this happened, Thor would instinctively draw back. When he replied to Fernando, it was always in a calm, unemotional manner. This was exasperating for Fernando. He would lean forward in another attempt to engage Thor in passionate debate. Equally firmly, Thor would again draw back. Thor started to regard Fernando as pushy and argumentative; Fernando, for his part, began to view Thor as cold and aloof. The gap between them widened dramatically. The joint realization that their negotiations were going nowhere was viewed with gloomy satisfaction by cynics in both companies. If such senior people as Fernando and Thor couldn't work together then what chance was there for Trolltind and Ibanez? Perhaps it was better to suspend their joint venture for the time being. After all, they could always return to it later ... couldn't they?

In this brief and simple example of culture at work on an interpersonal level, what has happened? Thor and Fernando found they couldn't work together and because of this it was inferred that their respective companies couldn't work together. The proposed joint venture was indefinitely postponed. A strategic alliance never happened. Considerable commercial opportunities were lost.

But why couldn't Thor and Fernando work together? It's temptingly easy merely to shrug one's shoulders and cite 'cultural differences' but this is as potentially misleading as it is imprecise. The real reason why they couldn't work together was, simply, body distance. The right body distance for Fernando was too close for Thor; the right body distance for Thor was too far for Fernando. As a result of this behavioural imbalance, other behavioural differences such as speed and delivery of speech became magnified and distorted. The next step was interpersonal stereotyping, with such notions as 'pushiness' and 'aloofness'. From there, it's only one more short step to cultural stereotyping – 'fiery Latins' versus 'cold Nordic types'.

The imbalance was behavioural. But why did this imbalance exist? It existed because both parties had (conflicting) assumptions about the correct body distance to ntain. Both sets of assumptions were implicit in their respective behaviours. her Fernando nor Thor had ever questioned whether their assumptions on this er were correct; still less had they considered that people of different nationalities might have different and potentially conflicting ideas about what constituted correct body distance. All they knew was that they could not work together; they did not know why. And because they never knew why, they were wholly unable to learn from their experience. Sadly, this happens all the time.

A DEFINITION OF CULTURE

In recent years there have been many less than adequate definitions of organizational culture – particularly in management books about change. A widely touted definition of organizational culture is 'the way we do things here'. However, the most cursory inspection of this definition shows that it is seriously lacking. 'The way we do things here' refers, literally, to behaviour. Certainly, Thor and Fernando had behavioural problems but they were caused by cultural differences, and because the problems were cultural in origin both Fernando and Thor were unaware of their true source.

My definition of culture is simple. Culture is, in general, **implicit assumption**, in particular, **the set of assumptions implicit in behaviour**. Thor and Fernando held different assumptions about correct body distance. It was precisely because these were assumptions that neither person was aware of them. And yet these assumptions had the power to create immense behavioural problems. To a large extent, the power of culture is derived from its implicit aspect. In order to change culture, the implicit must be made explicit – and resolved. This is particularly difficult due to the obvious problem of identifying what is implicit in the first place.

HOW CULTURE IS FORMED

How does culture – particularly corporate culture – arise? Let's take a hypothetical example. Imagine a company beginning operations on a greenfield site. It matters not a jot what the company does or where it is. All we need to know is that, each day, people come in to work. Products are made and sold; the company operates in a traditional business manner. Because the company started on a greenfield site, there was no existing tradition, history or culture. All these had to be created. Of the people who came to work on the site, some knew each other previously; many were unacquainted.

Within days of the site opening, quite distinct **behavioural norms** began to be developed. People called each other Jim or Bella, as distinct from Mr Smith or Mrs Thornton. Generally speaking, people came to work and left on time; punctuality was valued. Meal breaks, however, were rarely adhered to and workers routinely absented themselves from the shop floor without consulting supervisors. From the outset, production was uneven; there was a pronounced month-end syndrome as people frenetically struggled to catch up on their output targets.

These behavioural norms of formality, punctuality, discipline and output were accompanied by similar norms relating to almost every other type of behaviour. To a certain extent these behavioural norms were specific to particular departments and work groups, but to a large extent they were company-wide. It was frustratingly diffi- cult, for example, for the technical librarian to become known as Mrs Thornton when the managing director was known to all and sundry as plain 'Jim'.

There are two highly interesting points about behavioural norms. The first point is that they arise relatively quickly – in hours and days, rather than weeks or months. The second point is that people are highly aware of them.

Think back to your first days at a new school. You very rapidly (and often painfully) learned specific behavioural norms. You learned – literally – what was expected of you. Graphically, this is depicted by Figure 1. 'If I do this (**behaviour**), then the consequent effect (**result**) will follow. I now expect this to happen (**expectation**).'

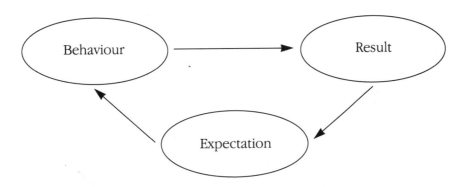

FIGURE 1   THE DEVELOPMENT OF EXPECTATION

Thus, at our greenfield site, if I start to ask what are regarded as awkward questions (behaviour), social disapproval quickly follows (result). I now expect this to happen (expectation). So I learn not to ask awkward questions. My learning is at the level of expectation. I've learned – quickly and consciously. Ouch!

Now, let's imagine that many months, perhaps even a year, have passed. With each behavioural norm, we have gone through the behaviour/result/expectation loop many times. We now find that a new factor has emerged – one which we call '**attitude**'. We may depict this by Figure 2. Whereas expectation formed part of a first order loop, attitude is part of a second order loop.

How then does attitude differ from expectation? Well, let's reconsider the two key points about expectation. Whereas expectation arose relatively quickly (hours/days), attitude took much longer to form (months/a year). Whereas we are highly aware of

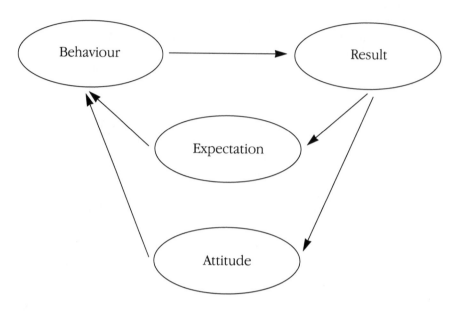

FIGURE 2   THE DEVELOPMENT OF ATTITUDE

expectation, we are much less aware of attitude. With attitude, we are starting to take things for granted.

Let's go back to our greenfield site. Now many, many years have passed. Everybody has gone through the first-order loop (behaviour/result/expectation) innumerable times. They have also gone through the second-order loop (behaviour/result/attitude) innumerable times. The behaviour which was enshrined in behavioural norms has now become enshrined in attitudinal norms – of which people are but dimly aware.

Without noticing it, another element has emerged. This we call **culture**. It is illustrated in Figure 3.

How does culture differ from attitude? Again, let's reconsider the two key points relating to time and awareness. Attitude arose over months/a year; culture arose over many years. And whereas we are dimly aware of attitude, we are almost entirely unaware of culture.

Let's go back to a piece of original behaviour – the asking of awkward questions. At the expectation level, we were highly aware that we shouldn't ask them. At the attitude level, we were only dimly aware that we shouldn't ask them – we just didn't, that's all. But at the culture level, it wouldn't even occur to us to ask awkward questions. We would have implicitly assumed that they should not be asked (as did Thor and Fernando). And if we encountered someone such as a newcomer to the company who did not share our implicit assumptions, we would probably be deeply offended – without quite knowing why.

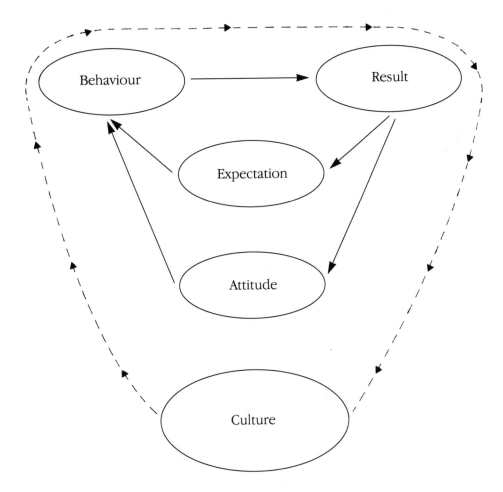

FIGURE 3   THE DEVELOPMENT OF CULTURE

And those other behavioural norms? Yes, they're all enshrined in our culture. Everybody is routinely called by their first name. (That snooty Mrs Thornton never did fit in and left a long time ago.) People come and go, according to the clock. Unfortunately, they do little else but clockwatch when they are at work. Meal breaks are never that little bit too short, always that little bit too long. It always takes three girls for one to go to the toilet. Those month-end syndromes create output curves steeper than the north face of the Eiger.

And what can be done? Just try and change any of these cultural norms and see what happens – like the ill-fated Mrs Thornton, you too may find that you're no longer around.

What we have learned so far can be summarized by reference to Table 1.

TABLE 1   THE DIMENSIONS OF EXPECTATION, ATTITUDE AND CULTURE

Variable	Timescale	Awareness
Expectation	Hours/days	Highly aware
Attitude	Months/a year	Dimly aware
Culture	Many years	Unaware

Having defined culture and shown how it arises, we now need to consider the concept of change.

THE CONCEPT OF CHANGE

As stated in the Preface, change is simultaneously one of the great themes and clichés of our time. Pick up a newspaper or magazine and you read about change. Switch on the television and you hear about change. But, for me, there is always a little problem associated with change. We use the word all the time without ever thinking about what it means, which is why it's a cliché. I have never heard anyone successfully define it. Have you?

My chosen profession is management consultancy. Many, if not most, management consultants blandly describe themselves as agents of change, but when I ask them to define what they mean by change, they tend to exhibit one of two reactions. Either they become highly uncomfortable and overtly defensive or they wax lyrically and verbiosely on the subject. Both reactions seem very much like avoidance of reality.

Change is an uncomfortable reality – make no mistake about that. For a start, there are no obvious synonyms of change which do justice to the concept. When a word has no obvious synonyms, it is likely that the word is a pivotal concept. This is the case with change. It is a pivotal concept which is greatly misunderstood and which is of immense importance in our world. Let's take a practical example of change and see whether we can arrive at a sound working definition.

AN EXAMPLE OF CHANGE

Nearly everybody has heard of the Leaning Tower of Pisa. Very few of us know who built it or what the circumstances were. Equally few of us have any idea as to why it is leaning. All we know is that it does lean – and at a considerable angle. In fact, it leans more than any other building we could mention.

Let's assume (and, for all I know, this may be the case) that each year the Leaning Tower of Pisa leans just a little bit more – perhaps a tenth of an inch. The naked eye cannot discern any difference but relevant instrumentation tells us that the angle of tilt has definitely increased this year.

Is this change? Well, we could probably have a lengthy and highly unproductive debate on the subject. A few people might argue that it was change. Most people, I suspect, would say it wasn't.

Now let's take another scenario. The tower is sitting there as before, tilting away much as it has always tilted (oh, all right then, just a little bit more). Is this change? Forget it! Suddenly, out of the dark of night, comes a terrible storm, a storm such as has not been seen before and will not be seen again. The storm strikes the great Tower of Pisa. And, lo and behold, it collapses.

Instantly the Leaning Tower of Pisa is world news. It is flashed on to hundreds of millions of television screens from Seattle to Mongolia. Households in Dingle, in Aix-en-Provence, in Iquitos, are invaded by its image. At the press of a button we learn who built the tower and why it tilted. Histories of the tower are hurriedly reissued; new ones are rushed into print. Soon, it seems, practically everybody on the planet knows about the tower and what has happened.

A DEFINITION OF CHANGE

Is this change? Certainly it is. But why is it change? After all, the tower was already in a state of transition. It was already tilting when the storm struck it.

Clearly change is about difference, specifically difference through time. For each of the preceding years, the tower was different from the year before. But the difference wasn't significant. Now the difference is significant and so we have what we call change.

Thus a technical definition of change might be **significant difference**. That certainly works in the example above and, if you think of a few examples yourself, I think you'll find that it works in them too. However, if we left the definition there, we would have missed half of it, and, I believe, the more important half. For which are more important – technical definitions or those which are applicable to our everyday world?

The real power of change is that it is **the experience of significant difference**. Consider, for a moment, about the feelings of shock, of outrage, of dismay felt by all those people watching their television screens. Before, they hadn't given a thought about the Leaning Tower of Pisa for years; now each of them feels that he or she has personally lost something of value. Irrational maybe. But true, none the less.

Think of a change in your own life – the death of a loved one, the end of a relationship. Recall the turmoil in your mind and body. Remember how 'you weren't yourself', how many weeks and months went by before you really came to terms with it.

These were sad changes. Yet you also feel turmoil at happy changes in your life. Remember the terrible excitment as a child when you won a worthwhile prize. Recall the power and intensity of your feelings when your first child was born. Suddenly the world seemed a different place. There were no words which could adequately describe your experience.

Change is the experience of significant difference. It is, above all else, experience. Experiences are personal, individual. My experience of the same event may be wildly different from yours. For example, you may find a radical comedienne deeply offensive, whereas I, with admittedly lower tastes, think she is absolutely hilarious.

Thus, people's responses to what is supposed to be the same change may be very different. For one person, redundancy may be the chance to do what they have always wanted; for many others, it is the entrance ticket to a living hell. It is fatal to assume that people's experiences of the same event are identical. Unfortunately that tends to be exactly what is assumed when it comes to corporate culture change. By denying the validity of personal experience, dragon's teeth are sown. Their bitter harvest is that well-known phenomenon – resistance to change.

But why do organizations need to change at all?

ORGANIZATIONS AS CLOSED SYSTEMS

A useful approach to organizations is to consider them as closed systems. This approach applies to all organizations whether private companies, public bureaucracies, profit making or non-profit making. This approach is shown in Figure 4.

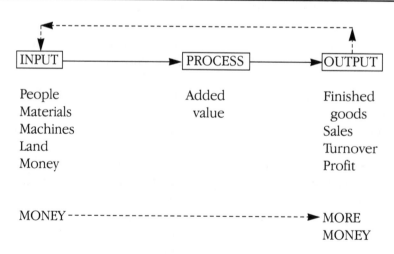

FIGURE 4   AN ORGANIZATIONAL CLOSED SYSTEM

The example shown in Figure 4 obviously relates to a profit-making organization. Here the goal of the company is to use money to make more money. The initial investment is converted into factors of production, specific inputs, such as raw materials. These inputs are then transformed into outputs which are worth more, i.e. *value has been added* as, for instance, when raw materials become finished goods. Obviously the goods have to be sold so, even in the closed system, there is life beyond the factory. In the past, however, particularly in niche markets with a few favoured customers, this model of a company was a fairly accurate one. There was a comforting sense of security amid the workforce. You knew what your company stood for, and why you were there. You were a shipbuilder, an airline worker, a baker. Working life may not have been easy (it rarely is) but at least the parameters were known. For many people in many industries life simply went on as before. Next year would be similar to last year and change was for someone else.

The model is as easily applicable to the public sector as it is to the private sector. Here though, the simple goal of using money to make more money would probably be unsuitable. Instead, the process of transformation would most likely be one of *added social value* such as helping drug users to change their habits for more productive and happier lives.

A closed system model of an organization is simple, rational and highly useful. However, it is also utterly inadequate. It is inadequate because the workings of a modern organization are not self-contained in the way that the workings of a central heating system are self-contained. They are not sealed. They interact with the outside world.

Thus we need to consider organizations in terms of open systems. This approach is shown in Figure 5.

Ironically, the open systems view of organizations encompasses the closed system view. As before, the company is transforming inputs into outputs at an operational level but, at a strategic level, the organization is merely one planet among many in a potentially vast universe. In this universe, however, the planets are free to interact with each other.

This may sound terribly theoretical, yet several years ago, a then household name British airline was hit in the same year by three separate global disasters, none of which it had anticipated. First it lost money in Africa. Second it was adversely affected by currency exchange rates, and third the Chernobyl disaster removed its transatlantic tourist trade. Lady Bracknell memorably remarked that, while to lose one parent could be regarded as a misfortune, to lose both looked like carelessness. Similarly, very few organizations are prepared to regard themselves in terms of open systems and ask such anxiety-provoking questions as 'Our business depends upon factors X, Y and Z. What could affect these factors, when, how and by how much? What would we do then? What could we do now, to avoid such situations in the first place?' To ignore strategy is to be a punter. The aforesaid airline, sadly, was weakened, taken over and lost its distinctive identity. Many of its employees, whom I had known and liked, lost their jobs.

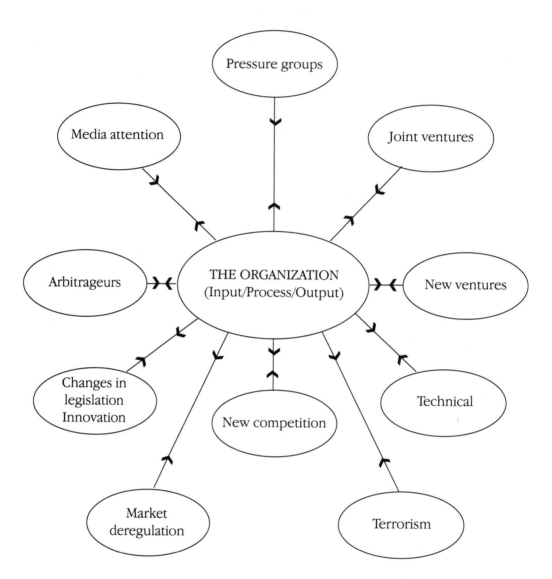

FIGURE 5   ORGANIZATIONS AS OPEN SYSTEMS

Similarly, the company secretary of a leading British printing concern was settling down to his coffee one morning several years ago, when his equanimity was disturbed by the brusque intrusion of an unexpected visitor.

'Look here, I'm terribly sorry to barge in on you like this,' the newcomer began, civilly enough. 'I know we've not met, but ... my company's just put in a bid for yours.'

With that, he pushed some documentation into the startled executive's hand and departed whence he came.

Thus started one of the most bitter takeover battles in British industrial history. All the more surprising then that the name of the aggressor company (a bitter rival) was totally unknown to the company secretary. Ignore open systems for long enough and you too will become history.

And yet people do ignore open systems – and for compelling reasons. For a start, most of the workforce (managers included) spend much of their working lives deep within closed systems, concerned with the problems of their department, their work group, their shift, their little part of the factory. And to hell with the rest!

While one might wish that each member of an organization would be concerned with the greater good of the organization, in reality, considerable sub-optimization usually happens. At director level, the break between closed and open systems is supposed to occur, directors being specifically charged with the greater good of the organization. How many directors truly fulfil this role? In my experience, very, very few. Most operate as glorified department heads. After all, their departments (and the closed system) are where they have come from. Also, many managers operate at one or more levels below their supposed capacity, i.e. they continue to do what they were once good at. At managing director/chairman level, the situation is usually rather better. Nevertheless it is temptingly easy to be dragged down to an operational level (closed system) rather than remain at a strategic level (open system). Even when chairmen and managing directors are alert, to make progress requires alertness on a team basis rather than an individual one.

A classic way to analyse a company is in terms of a SWOT (Strengths/ Weaknesses/Opportunities/Threats) analysis. Strengths and weaknesses belong to the organization itself, the closed system; opportunities and threats belong to the environment, the open system. The promise of the open system is that the greatest chances for success will come from it; the downside is that from the same open system will come unseen, unsuspected forces which, if undetected for long enough, will put you out of business.

People ignore the open system because they were brought up in the closed system. They continue to ignore the open system because their power base is in the closed system. They also ignore the open system because it requires the creativity of divergent thinking – and most managers are sharply convergent thinkers. They ignore the open system because time spent 'just thinking' is difficult to justify to themselves and others. And, most of all, they ignore the open system because it is so frightening.

It's frightening to realize that you're just one tiny planet in a vast universe, which, most of the time, looks as if it's trying to punish you personally. It's frightening to know that, much as you might like to, you have little control over events in that universe. It's frightening to feel that somewhere out there, beyond your ken, hostile powers are watching your every move while plotting their own.

It is a strange fact of life that opportunities in the open system are far outweighed by threats. Many of the examples given above of open system elements, such as legislation, pressure groups and terrorism, are rarely revenue generating. Usually they consume revenue. However, if you ignore them, you're not being a gambler (which is what all true businesspeople are), you're being a punter. Sooner or later, your time too will be up.

Corporate heads often become fixated on one or two elements of the open system, to the detriment of others. In recent years, we have seen considerable attention paid to elements such as quality and environmentalism by companies who formerly couldn't give a damn about either. The more your attention span is filled, the greater the blind spot being developed and that blind spot is potentially fatal.

While all companies inhabit a global village which is itself part of a greater open system, what matters for each company is that it identifies its personal open system. Each personal open system will be as unique as an individual's fingerprint or genetic code. This is why corporate success factors need to be individually determined.

The hard part of strategic analysis lies in the identification of which elements of the open system are truly significant. This is a slippery business which is all too easy to misjudge. But, if the assessment is correct and the truly significant elements have been identified, then the easy part of change management is over. Each significant element in the open system is an equally significant imperative for change.

We can now return to our original question and answer it. Organizations need to change because elements in the open system force them to change – or else play Russian roulette.

THE LEAD TIME OF CULTURE CHANGE

We defined change as '**the experience of significant difference**'. Strategic analysis is not change management. Change cannot be achieved by merely talking about it any more than oral sex is talking about sex. Thus the vital ingredient of change is action. Without action, there is no change. Without sustained action, there is no sustainable change. Without action which is progress, there is no worthwhile change. These are simple truths which many ignore.

A useful model of organization which neatly dovetails with the systems models is shown in Figure 6. The operational level encompasses all of an organization's operations, not just production, i.e. marketing, technical, finance, etc. – whatever people work at. In a private sector company, this level is engaged in wealth creation. In fact, only a subset of that level – direct labour – is making money. The rest of us are overheads. That doesn't matter as long as we genuinely earn our keep. If we do not genuinely earn our keep then it does matter, for we are being kept by our fellow workers and/or our customers. Inevitably, this applies to the next two levels which are also overheads.

The organizational level encompasses all managers from first-line supervisor to department head. Their collective role is to manage the closed system.

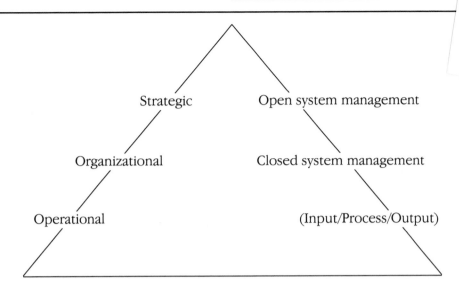

FIGURE 6   LEVELS OF ORGANIZATION

The strategic level is, in the private sector, company directors, managing directors and company chairmen, together with certain of their advisers. Their collective role is to balance the closed system with the open system so that continued profitability is achieved.

Let's imagine that a particular element in the open system is acting as an imperative for change. For example, due to deregulation, a company has lost its favoured niche market status. The good days are over. Now it must dramatically improve efficiency to survive.

The company will probably have to decrease overheads and increase productivity throughout the closed system. Without strong leadership from the top, it may well do neither. Instead, people may talk about change rather than make it. This is a classic first line of defence.

However, if strong leadership from the top exists, there is a strategic choice of change implementation. Should it be top-down or bottom-up? If it's top-down then, like trickle-down economics, what trickles down into operational benefit is likely to be scanty. If it's bottom-up, then it is usually comparatively easy to achieve, or appear to achieve, operational change at or around the shop floor where people are conditioned to do what they're told. But change here is apt to be short-lived. It is often frustrated by the organizational level, which typically feels that it is under fire from above and below.

In enabling change to happen, the vital skills, as many functional specialists painfully learn, are organizational, not operational. Top-down change will be blocked by the organization; bottom-up change will be stifled by it. The most enthusiastic quality circle team leaders become the most disillusioned when they progress from minor operational change to more significant operational changes which affect the organizational level. Ouch! Those glass ceilings really hurt!

At a conscious level, people in organizations act to retain the status quo and thus avoid change; at an unconscious cultural level, they also do so. The unconscious level is, by far, the more powerful. At the conscious level people are protecting rational interests like status and job security. At the unconscious level they are protecting their psyches. People will die to protect their psyches.

Remember our fictitious organization, the one in which behaviour and results begat expectation, attitude and culture? Corporate change, if it is to mean anything of value, must involve sustained action, i.e. altered behaviour and results. The whole point of change is to achieve progress, i.e. better results. As Marlene Dietrich remarked to Ernest Hemingway, 'Never confuse action with progress.'

The problem is that when you try to change behaviour to obtain different results, it seems that the entire culture acts to frustrate your efforts. People who have been in this situation will readily testify to the mind-numbing qualities of frustration which lie in wait for the inexperienced. You plough on, trying your best to ensure that what you regard is right actually happens. But it's like floundering in thick mud; with each step taken it seems as if you've slipped three-quarters of a step back. The harder you try, the heavier are the forces of inertia against which you have to push. The personal cost in expended energy becomes enormous. Now it's like swimming the butterfly stroke through treacle. Culture seems to be acting as a vast, ponderous counterweight, making a mockery of all your efforts.

In truth, culture does act as a counterweight which continually operates to keep the organization in a state of equilibrium – the status quo. This makes very good sense. Without this mechanism to protect organizations they would be in such a state of constant flux that purposeful work or even psychological existence would be impossible. Each novel stimulus would drive them off course.

Have you ever met a person with a butterfly mind, who never seems to start or finish anything? Instead they leap from subject to subject in a constant search for novelty and distraction. After ten minutes with them you feel that you too no longer know what you're doing. You need to get away from them, sit down and work out what you were supposed to be doing in the first place. Only then do you feel that you're back on an even keel. Without culture, organizational life would be like that, only worse. It would be a perpetual madhouse. Culture preserves the status quo, psychological and otherwise, and that is an indispensable function.

Inevitably, however, in preserving the status quo, culture acts to negate change. The more one tries to accomplish change the greater the opposing forces of inertia. This will happen partly at a conscious level but to a large extent it will also happen at a subconscious level. And it is the subconscious level which, as the example of Thor and Fernando revealed, has such power.

If an element in the open system is acting as an imperative for change, only when there is a genuine, sustained difference in behaviour and results can change be said to have occurred. The potentially awesome power of culture will act to frustrate change. And, from whatever direction change comes, the organizational level will almost certainly block progress.

For such an organization, the lead time of cultural change will be all important. This is the time from emergence of the force for change in the environment through to detection and successful implementation of new behaviour and results. If this lead time is too long then the organization is in trouble. If the change is vital, the organization may not survive.

WAYS OF ATTEMPTING TO BRING ABOUT CHANGE

There are three traditional ways of attempting to bring about change:

O   Rational discussion
O   Power
O   Hearts and minds

Their respective strengths and weaknesses will be examined in turn.

RATIONAL DISCUSSION

If there is an imperative for change and the organization needs to respond then surely there will be a valid, rational argument for change? Why not communicate this argument, formulate suitable plans and then implement them? Change will occur.

This may be what should happen but in practice it never does happen – at work or elsewhere. Think of the last time you persuaded your partner or children to change after exposure to your, oh, so rational arguments? Think of the last time you permanently lost weight, drank less and exercised because there was a good reason, a rational argument for so doing?

At work, rational argument for change usually ignores two key factors. One factor, politics, is at least semi-conscious and thus semi-visible (although beware being too sure of yourself here, lest you share the fate of Caesar). Always there will be a political status quo of vested interest. Somebody's power and status will be threatened as, for instance, when operational power is devolved to the shop floor. Potentially worse, differentials may be threatened. ('If you've made them stronger and we're unchanged, then we're weaker.' Well, relatively.... But, for many people, differentials are more important than absolutes.) Political interest operates on a rather different level from rational discussion. Rational discussion may elicit what appears to be best for the company. Political interest deals with what you and I selfishly perceive to be best for us. Our perceptions may be quite misguided. I may be utterly incompetent and a liability to the company. My political views may suffer from short-termism, and sub-optimization; yours may be no better. Acquiring what we want may involve unfair disadvantages for other colleagues and work groups. So what? As long as our best interests are served....

Organizational politics, which is inevitable and omnipresent, is power without responsibility, the prerogative of the harlot. Whatever else it does, it does not add value. Unless managed, it will effortlessly block, stifle, circumvent or negate rational discussion.

The other factor, if it were needed, which has the power to reduce rational discussion to mush is culture. Culture acts to preserve psychological survival via maintenance of the status quo and thus, regardless of whether the proposed change is good or bad, culture will automatically seek to negate it. Because culture is largely unconscious and unseen, most people don't, as with politics, have to choose sides; they are automatically on the opposing side.

Change via rational discussion? Forget it! The chance would be a fine thing. Try again.

POWER

Few of us are megalomaniacs who enjoy wielding power for the sheer fun of it. Most of us expect to achieve what we want through providing good reasons why we should have it, i.e. rational discussion. But, if rational discussion doesn't do the trick, what then?

This situation is particularly applicable to people brought in to change companies and other organizations. If they have had previous experience of change management then, if nothing else, they will know that rational discussion will not of itself work. There is an almost overwhelming temptation simply to use power. This can vary from the strikingly unsubtle autocratic management which formerly characterized British management to 'the honey tongue and weasel words' which a client of mine once mentioned. (I'm sure he was referring to somebody else!)

Once more, however, the twin devils of politics and culture turn up irritatingly to frustrate. Power certainly carries more political clout than rationality. (It should do, as attainment of power is the aim of politics.) However, many chief executives have discovered to their horror that supposedly absolute power seems to enable them to achieve absolutely nothing of value.

This is unsurprising. Although a new chief executive may have considerable authority (legitimate power), other people in the organization may have far more clout in practice. Worse, in collusion, the synergy of other people's power may far outweigh that of the new chief executive. After all, they have had years in which to undertake their horse-trading, forge their alliances and form their power blocs. However talented, the new entrant is probably stepping into an established situation about which everyone else knows, but of which he or she is ignorant. And, of course, any battles will be conducted on their home turf.

Even in highly autocratic situations, the chief executive's authority may be insufficient. The colonial district commissioner often found that his godlike authority was no match for the wily natives. The prison governor of today may find, to his or her chagrin, that a particular inmate holds the aces in what is supposed to be the governor's prison.

Lacking an equivalent power base, the agent of change will often be struggling. The longer the honeymoon period, the greater the chance that she or he may be co-opted, made to go native, or shown up as incompetent and thus fit only for removal. Beware honeymoon periods! Time is on the side of the natives, or at least they will so assume. Therefore why provoke a conflict; why refuse to do your bidding? They don't need to say no; they can get away quite nicely with saying yes and making damn sure it never happens.

One of the classic ways of ensuring that what should happen doesn't is the withholding of information. Another client of mine once remarked, 'The whole management structure in this company acts as a giant, inverted sieve. It's got only one purpose – to filter out information and make sure it never reaches Bob. He thinks he knows what's going on but he doesn't know the half of it.' (Sad to say, my client occupied a key position in this very structure.)

Without information, it is impossible for a chief executive to find out what's happening. Equally, being swamped in routine information (another popular ploy) has the same effect. What our incumbent chief executive desperately needs is management control information, as distinct from mere management information.

The terms MCS (Management Control Systems) and MIS (Management Information Systems) tend to be used interchangeably. Not suprisingly, much confusion ensues and thus it is worth dwelling upon the difference between the two.

As noted earlier, all organizations exist to sustain operations which cannot be sustained by an individual. All operations can be characterized by closed system activity. Thus all operations are processes of conversion of inputs to outputs. This was first shown in Figure 4. An abbreviated form is shown in Figure 7.

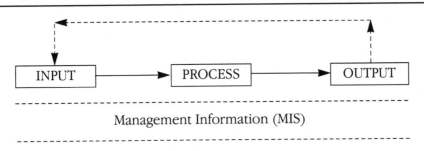

Management Information (MIS)

FIGURE 7   MANAGEMENT INFORMATION SYSTEMS

Anyone who has performed clerical work in an office will testify to the vast amount of documentation that most organizations seemingly need in order to conduct their business. Jokes are routinely made about cutting down Amazonian rainforests. Usually there is a partly manual, largely automated paper trail from first input to final output.

This is a management information system. Although it stretches from first input to final output, most of it will, in practice, deal with minute subdivisions of the process. As such, although it may be interesting to someone involved in such a subdivision, it tends to be uninteresting to anyone else. It's the sort of information which, when it spews out of the computer and lands on your desk (because, through status, you're on a circulation list), prompts the reaction, 'So what?' To the chap in the subdivision, it's information; to you, it's data – boring data at that.

The situation in Figure 8, however, is somewhat different. This tells us rather different stories. If the input is time, it tells us how many widgets were made in a shift, how many orders were despatched on schedule, how many customers have paid within the agreed credit period. The press of a button can give us the converse – how many (and what proportion) of widgets are we behind on, how many (and what proportion) of orders were despatched late, how many (and what proportion) of customers are tardy in paying.

$$\text{Operational index} \quad = \quad \frac{\text{OUTPUT}}{\text{INPUT}}$$

FIGURE 8   MANAGEMENT CONTROL SYSTEMS

Inspection of other outputs against inputs may reveal actual spend compared with budget (thus prompting investigation of variance), actual sales versus planned sales, and yearly return on capital versus target. Here we are obviously comparing actual results with planned results.

Management information is data to the non-specialist – boring data to be passively recorded. Management control information, however, always prompts – or should prompt – a decision. Are people satisfied with a particular situation? If not, what are they going to do about it? Management control information is the precursor to management decision and resulting action.

Usually organizations have a mixture of MIS and MCS. Almost always this leads to overproduction of MIS and gaps in the MCS. Thus, as a manager, I may receive volumes of outputs of MIS which I do not need and yet ironically fail to receive the relatively few MCS operational indices which I do need.

MCS operates at a higher order level than MIS. Whereas MIS only provides information to the specialist, MCS gives information to everyone. It is imperative that people receive MCS. It is also imperative that MCS is a true system, holistically encompassing every part of an organization, from bottom to top. MCS architecture can look formidable. In essence, what it seeks to do can be shown in Figure 9.

Interposing MCS between behaviour and results in an organization is one of only two ways to determine what is really going on. The other way is physically to go out

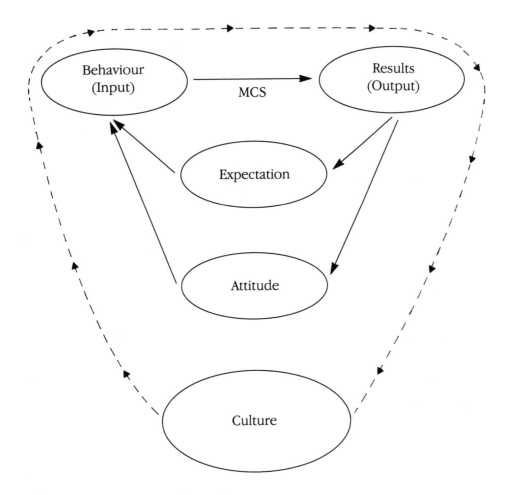

FIGURE 9   THE POWER OF MCS

and see for yourself. Complete understanding is only possible with personal experience of what is happening with the process, allied to possession of MCS operational indices of output/input. Figure 10 illustrates this fact.

Unfortunately, a chief executive or any other newcomer will find it difficult to discover what is happening in an organization through personal experience. Simple logistics dictate otherwise. After all, they are but one among very many indeed and, in practice, they will be forced into the alternative – numerical information.

Management control systems will therefore need to be interposed between behaviour and results at an operational level in the company. All systems, particularly inherited ones, suffer from data unreliability. The integrity of the numerical information

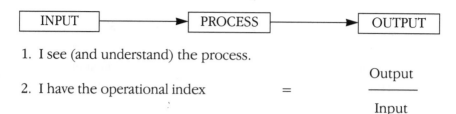

FIGURE 10   COMPLETE UNDERSTANDING OF A PROCESS

needs to be validated against relevant experience. On Shift 3, for example, the figures say we made X with Y and achieved a performance rating of Z. Is this what actually happened? If not, then what did happen, and why did it happen, and how was something else reported? If it did happen, then was it as good or as bad a result as the numbers suggest? Should X, Y or Z have been higher or lower? What were the real problems? How were they dealt with?

Installing management control systems is the best way that I know of quickly getting a grip on what is happening in a company. However, there are two caveats. Initially, systems will inevitably suffer from data unreliability. It is also essential to consider the way in which they are introduced – for this is a change in itself. If they are forced into place, they will be resented, strenuously opposed and will require rigorous policing to keep them intact. This is hardly a sound state of affairs. The prevailing management style cannot then be other than autocratic and people will become obsessive about covering up real or imagined mistakes.

If management control systems are developed by the users instead of foisted upon them, a different story will ensue. But this requires an incoming change agent to display trust in people, which few do.

The physicist Heisenberg noted that we affect what we study. In creating systems to find out what is occurring, we run the risk of causing immense resistance. This resistance will inhibit future change. The organization's flexibility in response to its environment will thus be severely diminished. Is that what we really want?

So, without information, we don't know what is really happening. Therefore we cannot make a proper assessment. In order to obtain information we have to assemble a management control system and in so doing we shall be heading straight into change – without assessment. A 'dammed if you do it, dammed if you don't' situation.

Because culture acts to preserve the status quo, arrivals are often viewed as culture attackers. They are then sternly resisted by culture defenders. Stereotypical accusations will flow: 'These people aren't living in the real world'; 'What does she know about running a television station?'; 'He's just a glorified accountant'; 'Cost savings must be made'; 'Quality ... what do those people care about quality?' The situation is shown in Figure 11.

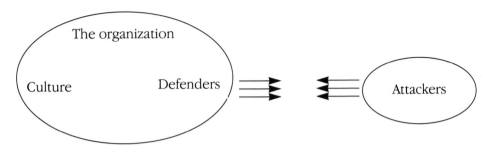

FIGURE 11   CULTURE ATTACKERS AND CULTURE DEFENDERS

In no way do I wish to suggest that it is impossible to create change through the deployment of power. It is possible to create change through power, as the experiences of many organizations will testify. The catch is this: because resistance to change will be at its maximum, it is highly likely that the change which comes about will not be the change which you want, and/or the side-effects will be adverse. The organization may have been 'restructured' but your workforce may be thoroughly demoralized. Costs may be cut but so may initiative. Procedures may be in place but people may not give a damn about them.

In recessionary times, power-driven change is much in vogue and people accept it because they have mouths to feed and mortgages to pay. When they can vote with their feet, they will. Psychologically, they have probably already voted with their feet. You've lost them and they won't be back. Power-driven change rarely works.

HEARTS AND MINDS

We have good reasons for change. We know that rational discussion will not achieve it. We also know that power is apt to give rise to unpleasant side-effects. So we have to win people over – persuade them of our point of view.

This is how programmes of education begin. Employees whose exposure to management communication has hitherto been scanty are invited to communication sessions, briefings, seminars, workshops. The list seems endless, and it is. This is communication with a capital C. However, there's also a small c – a catch. People are not merely being invited to attend these sessions, they're expected to attend. Woe betide them if they do not. The invisible hand of power is still present but in a covert form. Instead of being told 'Do this', the message now is 'Come to my seminar'.

People are not fools. They may sometimes behave like fools, but believe me, they are not. They'll come to your seminar if they think they stand to gain and they'll listen to you if they think you're being honest with them. Otherwise – forget it!

If you set out to win people's hearts and minds, there are only two routes. The first is manipulation and, sadly, that is the route most frequently chosen. People will always be aware of it although, for personal protection, many will accept a temporary degree of self-illusion. Few will be convinced. Certainly, the Korean War demonstrated that people could be 're-educated' through brainwashing. Brainwashing, however, is scarcely a viable option in modern organizations.

The other way to win people's hearts and minds is for them to be freely given. This is genuine leadership. While leadership is often treated as a Holy Grail of management, few professional managers display convincing powers of leadership – at least the charismatic type of leadership which is necessary for people to give freely of their hearts and minds. Ironically, some unmitigated scoundrels display formidable levels of charismatic leadership. Well, at least they're human.

It's not impossible to win people's hearts and minds but true industrial leaders are few and far between. The forces of culture which shape our expectations and attitudes, which affect our conscious and unconscious minds, may be susceptible to an individual's leadership. It is, however, a slender chance.

WAYS OF ATTEMPTING TO BRING ABOUT CHANGE: AN ASSESS-MENT

The three most widely used methods of attempting to bring about change all have serious limitations. Rational discussion will rarely get very far. The winning of hearts and minds is only possible for the very few. The use of power will, almost inevitably, create undesirable side-effects. In addition, there is no guarantee that the changes which result are those which were originally envisaged.

By this point, it is probably impossible not to feel considerable discouragement. Many management books seem to suggest that there is an easy way to achieve results; this book emphatically does not. Rather, it suggests that there is no easy way for organizational culture to change. The sheer power of culture as a counterbalance against change is one opposing factor. There is another: too often, when we consider organizations, we view them in a way which is partly appropriate – and largely inappropriate.

THE SOCIAL REALITY OF ORGANIZATIONS

Sit down with any chief executive to discuss their organization and, sooner or later, she or he will pick up the telephone and ask their secretary to bring in a copy of the family tree – the organization chart. The top layer of a typical organization chart is shown in Figure 12.

Organization charts look reassuringly logical and sensible. If there is one word which, more than any other, sums up the attributes of an organization chart it is the word 'rational'.

What the chart does is split the organization into parts and arrange those parts in a hierarchy. It is thus a reductionist device – it views the whole as the sum of its parts.

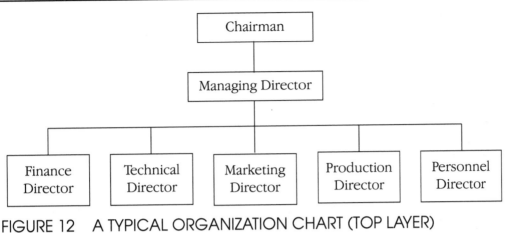

FIGURE 12   A TYPICAL ORGANIZATION CHART (TOP LAYER)

Naturally, organizations cannot be left to operate as vast amorphous masses; they need to be split into parts – usually in terms of function, occasionally in terms of product groupings.

But there are at least two dangers. The first is that, when you split an organization into parts, there are inevitable factional differences between these parts. The potential for conflict is always present. It is like dividing a country into a number of constituent states. As many members of organizations will testify, the 'them and us' battles which ensue can be particularly bloody.

The first difficulty with differentiation – splitting an organization into its constituent parts – is therefore integration. Often, the parts stubbornly refuse to fit neatly together. This is puzzling. We nervously laugh it off with phrases like 'Well, that's people for you', but it's still puzzling because the family tree – the organization chart – looks eminently rational. It explodes an organization into its parts, much as an engineering drawing explodes an internal combustion engine or a grandfather clock into parts and *they* certainly fit back together again with few problems of integration.

Let's imagine that we have a company, say a manufacturing site in the Midlands, split into the functional areas shown in Figure 12. Let's further imagine that the site is neatly divided into five geographical areas, each corresponding to a functional discipline. Suppose we colour code – one colour per function/geographical area. Finance is yellow, technical is green, marketing is blue, production is beige and personnel is pink. If we look at a model of the site, it is nicely subdivided into constituent coloured areas.

Now let's imagine that we have a computer graphics package which shows the site in terms of the colours which are present. Thus, when people come into work in the morning, production fills up with beige, as the early shift gets under way. Next there is a single speck of green in the technical area; the technical director comes in early. Soon, he's joined by three of his project engineers – more green. By half past eight, almost all of the functions/areas are glowing with their constituent colours.

With our package, each time a person from one function interacts with a person from another function, one colour is superimposed on another. Thus, when the sales manager talks with the production controller about disrupting his schedule to expedite a special, we have blue on beige. When the personnel officer meets with a works accountant to query an employee's tax coding, we have pink on yellow. An interdisciplinary quality circle has beige, green, blue and yellow – all superimposed.

At half past eight, our model of the factory will look like a coloured version of the organization chart. But by nine o'clock, the colours will have begun to run. By twenty to ten, the running will be pronounced. By half past eleven our graphics model of the organization will be unrecognizable from the half-past-eight model. Instead of neatly colour-coded functions, we will have a horrible mess of colours running into each other. Hundreds of interactions will have taken place. Deals will have been agreed, alliances formed, rumours invented, prized titbits of gossip exchanged. To chart these interactions behaviourally would be a task of extreme complexity. And, remember, this is only three hours in the life of an average organization.

So the second difficulty with our organization chart is that the very way in which we view organizations is partly appropriate and partly inappropriate. Certainly, we have to divide them into parts. There is no question about that. And it is easier to split them up than to put the pieces back together into an integrated whole which is working to the same end. At the superficial level of the organization chart, everything appears rational, like an engineering diagram of the interior of a grandfather clock. But the important difference is that the parts of a grandfather clock make relatively few, strictly rational, interactions with other parts. The parts of an organization – people – interact with each other on a frequent if not intermittent basis which may be spontaneous, even random. At an organizational level, it seems the very opposite of rational.

Of course, at an individual level, there are always motives behind our actions. For example, there was a definite reason for that quality group meeting – to reduce scrap in metalwork. But Jane and Geoffrey enjoy flirting with each other as much as they like discussing the introduction of merit pay. And Charlie and Will have an understanding which comes from being members of the same Lodge. Phil and Arthur are on the committee of the local pigeon fanciers club. Dorothy and Peter have common academic contacts from their respective MBA days. Eddie, Henry and George used to work for an engineering firm in Wolverhampton. Jimmy, Fred, Agnes and Billy never forget when they used to work down at 'the substation'. 'You couldn't believe what it was like in the winter. The drips on the end of your nose would freeze solid,' Billy still claims.

So the formal groupings of the organization chart do not take account of the informal groupings which always exist. The informal groupings, based upon shared meanings, rituals and values, are highly tribal and therefore powerful. We rarely take them into account. The complexity of these psychological networks is frightening.

This then is the social reality of life within any company or organization. Please note that I am not employing any supposedly arcane sociological devices. I am merely describing what really happens. Anyone who has worked in an organization will agree that my description is accurate.

An organization is not a piece of machinery to be taken apart and put together again. It does not have a culture which requires merely a few pokes with a screwdriver and a quick test with a micrometer screw gauge. It does have functional realities such as production which are supposedly rational but it also has social realities which are far less susceptible to rational understanding. Neither are they irrational although at times they may seem so. They might more properly be described as arational – not susceptible to conventional rational analysis and certainly not irrational. The true reasons behind social realities often remain frustratingly elusive. Jane, Charlie, Dorothy, Fred and Billy are understandable individually and collectively, but probably only by someone who can combine in-depth knowledge of social science with considerable understanding of the world. Is it necessary to understand this famous five? Yes – if they're part of a caucus which will act to ensure that your carefully drafted plans for change end up where they are deemed rightfully to belong – in the dustbin.

THE STAGES OF ORGANIZATIONAL LIFE

We have considered organizations in terms of open and closed systems. In terms of open systems, they must maintain a dynamic balance with their environment. In terms of closed systems, they must win the war of added value in transforming raw inputs to coveted outputs. Very often, in order to maintain the correct dynamic balance, they must react to forces for change in the environment. As we have seen, this is no easy business, for the culture will tend to act as a vast counterbalancing mechanism. But organizations can face forces for change from within as well as from outside. One of the greatest potential forces for change is size itself.

Let's imagine an organization starting up. What do we need? The very least that we need is an entrepreneur. Let's imagine we have such an entrepreneur. He works in conventional employment but he has spied (he thinks) a market niche. In this case, his market niche is making and fitting window blinds to order. So he moonlights. He obtains orders from housewives, makes the blinds himself in a rented garage which he uses as a workshop, and also fits them himself. He keeps his own books and he uses an old van for sales visits and delivery of raw materials and finished goods. So far so good.

A couple of years pass. The business is thriving. A market niche has been identified and is being exploited. Our entrepreneur is now working full time. His wife does the books, his father-in-law makes the blinds along with two lads, one of whom is a nephew. Our entrepreneur is sales- and customer-oriented, so he continues to deal with the housewives. He procures orders and he installs the blinds.

Five years later, there are eighty people operating from new premises in a development area. The business is now a limited company, with four directors; all started out on the shop floor.

This is a typical example of a pioneer company. Our pioneer is a man or a woman with a vision. In this case, the vision is to become the best blindmaker in Europe, 'the

Marks & Spencer of blinds' as the pioneer puts it. Managers are jacks of all trades. There is no nonsense about professional managers; all are prepared to pitch in and make blinds when necessary. Management control is interpersonal; because there are only a few managers, everyone knows who is pulling their weight and who isn't. Slackers get short shrift, for the business cannot afford slackers. So, in practice, management control is via either trust or fear. It's a web. At the centre of the web is the pioneer. Members of the web or inner circle are likely to be family or friends – people who knew the pioneer in his early days and were induced or cajoled into the business.

The pioneer organization is relatively simple with few overheads. Its strength lies in its operational flexibility. It can rapidly change direction in response to market demand. Pioneer organizations can turn around much faster than General Motors. Also, there is a sense of life, of emotion about the business, sometimes even of passion – the passion of dreams which come true.

Of course, pioneer organizations have drawbacks. They cannot afford mistakes, so control is autocratic. Beware the fate of those who fall foul of pioneers! Thin-skinned souls may leave, preferring to work in less of a madhouse. The pioneer may, in Hitlerian manner, drive the whole organization to ruin when stubbornness becomes obsession. There are no capital reserves and therefore one mistake may leave you in trouble with the banks. Two mistakes and it's serious trouble. Three mistakes and it's all over.

The sober fact is that most pioneer organizations fail. There is a legion of individual reasons – overtrading, bad timing, poor cost control, lost contracts. Capital would have given them another chance, but pioneer businesses are usually starved of capital.

Let's assume an organization has survived to the next stage. We now have a brick-works with two hundred and eighty people on the same site. Now there are fifteen managers – not four. The role has become more important than the job holder. What this means is that the present production director will tend to act in the same way as the previous production director. Neither will do what old Joe, the original production director, did during the good old pioneer days. The era of the professional manager has arrived.

Management is now by memo ('far too many of 'em' say the old timers). There are computer-printed production schedules where there used to be the backs of envelopes. There are rules and regulations and procedures. Above all, there are systems. It is for this reason that the second stage of organizational life is called the systems stage.

Systems are needed because the business is now of such a size that, without systems, chaos will result. The character of a systems organization is dissimilar to a pioneer organization. It is not just that the business has quantitatively changed, has merely got bigger. It has qualitatively changed also. There is less emotion and more reasoned argument. There is less fun but also less terror. In a pioneer organization, everybody tends to know each other. In a systems organization, this is rarely possible.

Where is the point of transition between a pioneer organization and systems organization? One cannot specify in terms of turnover because different industries have different levels of bought-in services. (A one-man company, for instance a commodity broker, can have a turnover of several millions – the same as an eighty-person manufacturing plant.) But, very roughly speaking, when sites have between one hundred and one hundred and fifty people, an organization tends to enter the systems phase.

Whereas in the pioneer phase managers stuck to the same company, if not the same industry, in the systems phase there is a much greater degree of managerial mobility. For instance, the production director of our brickworks was once the general manager of a foundry. The personnel officer (we never needed them before!) has experience of local government and the Milk Marketing Board. The freelance PR consultant who contracts to do eight days' work a year has dozens of other clients, spread across the industrial and commercial spectrum.

The systems organization is a much less parochial and insular place than the pioneer organization. This may be both good and bad. Before there was no doubt that people's loyalties lay with the company, if not with the founder personally. Now their loyalties may primarily be to their professions if not themselves. They are more likely to think, 'I'm a management accountant, first and foremost,' rather than, 'I'm a brickworks man, first and foremost.'

With the systems phase, we leave good old 'seat of the pants' management behind and enter a world where power belongs to the role ('the sales manager'), not the job holder (Fred). Rationality has replaced emotion. The headiness of organizational youth has been replaced by sober middle age. Each day, life, slowly, imperceptibly, begins to resemble a bureaucracy.

With the next stage of organizational life – the integrated phase – bureaucracy has firmly arrived. Now we have, for example, a large financial services company, a household name, operating out of a prominent British town which it dominates. Like Ancient Rome, it has an empire of colonies (in this case, subsidiaries) and outposts (branch offices). Again, like Ancient Rome, it has an emperor, senators, acolytes, courtiers and, yes, courtesans also.

Our integrated organization is a leading national company, a utility, a public sector domain. It employs thousands if not tens of thousands of workers. Now authority is almost entirely vested in role. The senators, inside their organization, appear omnipotent. Outside their organization they are grey men in grey suits. Organizational old age is near at hand; the pension schemes can be fabulous.

These three stages of organizational life are shown in Figure 13. Some typical characteristics of these three stages are shown in Table 2.

Obviously all organizations do not fit neatly into this model. Models, as tentative maps of reality, are useful up to a point. At the point where we begin perceptually to distort reality to fit the maps, they become counterproductive. However, these three stages of organizational life, like Shakespeare's seven ages of man, are generic. It will

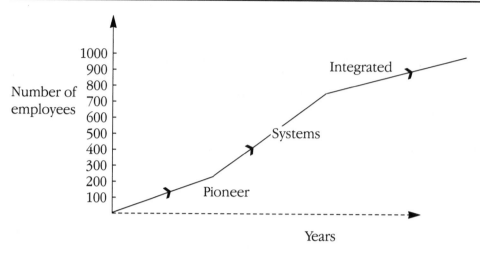

FIGURE 13   THE STAGES OF ORGANIZATIONAL LIFE

be surprising if there is not a significant degree of fit between your organization and one of these three life stages.

The point of this seeming digression into organizational growth is that, although imperatives for change will wing their way in from the environment, many organizations already face one of two possible crises of transition. When such transition is badly managed (and it usually is), the organization will be gravely weakened in the face of external threats.

The first crisis of transition is the change from pioneer to systems organization. Very often, this will have been delayed for many years because of a pioneer refusing to retire. It is easy to be disparaging about pioneers, forgetting that, without pioneers, we

TABLE 2   CHARACTERISTICS OF ORGANIZATIONAL LIFE

Stage	Management	Control	Motivation
Pioneer	Ad hoc Home grown	Interpersonal (Trust/Fear)	Entrepreneurial
Systems	Professional	Systems and procedures	Job satisfaction/ security
Integrated	Bureaucratic	Committee	Political

would still be living in caves. Their followers, rough diamonds many of them, evince a loyalty which will rarely be encountered elsewhere. But an organization which, by virtue of size or complexity, belongs in the systems phase, yet is staffed by pioneers, is an organization which will have acute problems of change. There will be a pronounced culture lag between business needs and people's values. There will be expediency rather than accountability. There will be firefighting rather than planning and smooth execution. In short, there will be rowdy adolescence where there needs to be responsible adulthood. Changing from pioneer to systems is a difficult task. The substance of the enterprise must alter and the spirit must be transformed, not stifled. Culture change must come about through delicacy and skill – not common brutality.

Often, a company's triumphant entrance into the systems phase is entry to a killing ground. Pioneer companies often have enviable flexibility. Markets change; they can also change. Integrated organizations act to dominate the infrastructure and guarantee their continued existence by political means – PR, pressure groups, trade associations, etc. Systems organizations are too big to be small and too small to be big. With contracting markets and fewer players, the choice may be stark: gobble up lesser fry or be swallowed up yourself.

Integrated organizations, like empires of old, are apt to sink under the collective weight of their own inertia. There are too many bright young things, too many MBAs, too many task forces, working parties, committee meetings. Above all, there are too many meetings. Panel interviews mean that we recruit 'people like us' and promote only those whom we deem to be 'a safe pair of hands'. Is it really any wonder that we end up with people who are disparagingly referred to as 'empty suits'?

As the great oligopolies of yesteryear fray and tear at the edges, there is a remorseless trend towards decentralization. The talk now is of devolving into business units, of a leaner, meaner head office, with fewer managerial layers and fewer divisions. (The not so secret agenda here is reduced overhead. Unless the organization sheds weight, it will go the way of the dinosaurs.)

Devolution into business units certainly seems to make sense. A site with three hundred people is apt to have much more flexibility than a site with fifteen hundred people. It can be more customer focused, perhaps even as customer focused as the pioneer organizations against which it may be competing. Unlike them, it has a corporate umbrella, is known to the public and has backing. As a customer, you may be paying a little more, but you are probably receiving a much higher level of professionalism. Business units, as parts of integrated organizations, do not fly by the seat of their pants. They have systems; they also have flexibility.

In many ways, the truly devolved business unit is ideal for business effectiveness and managerial satisfaction. The joy of being a manager is freedom multiplied by resources. If I work for a vast monolith which is not properly devolved, then I may have a budget of millions yet very little freedom in how I can use it. The result is not much job satisfaction. If I resign in disgust and start up a corner sweet shop, I may have great operational freedom (which should it be this week – lollipops or gobstoppers?), but very few resources (usually an unsympathetic bank manager). The result –

not much more job satisfaction. But, as MD of a devolved business, with a budget of several millions and the simple (!) requirement to turn in a return on capital of 17 per cent, I may discover enormous fulfilment.

The problem is that the people who run devolved business units are usually the same people who served their time with the vast monoliths which spawn devolved business units. They joined the company because they wanted security. They were accepted and favoured over less tame colleagues. Creativity ebbed from them as they groomed and were groomed for highly political senior management roles, where playing not to lose was far more important than playing to win. Executive perks and the glorious pension scheme acted as bromide to already flagging managerial libidos. And now, to cut loose as the MD of a business unit? 'Super idea, Giles.' ('But, my God, it's everything I've fought to avoid.')

The development of truly devolved, integrated organizations requires replacing low-risk, medium-reward norms by high-risk, high-reward ones. Whatever the nature of individual cultures, there will be huge cultural shifts involved, shifts which will be fought tooth and nail by powerful groups of threatened employees. Culture attack and defence will be very much in play. The new hard man or woman who has been brought in for 'restructuring' will have notable enemies.

Many organizations in Britain and abroad are struggling and will continue to struggle with the transformation between pioneer and systems or between systems and integrated. The commonly used, absurdly short-term, 'change programmes' tend to be simplistic solutions to complex problems. Fifty years of history cannot be conveniently dismissed with a few briefing seminars and workshops. Would that life were so simple. And, while you painfully struggle to put your house in order, ravenous wolves are already howling at the gates.

CULTURE AND CHANGE: A SUMMARY

We have defined culture and we have defined change. We have learned that neither is straightforward. We have further learned that changing culture is fraught with difficulty. Yet many organizations have cultures which are acutely dysfunctional. Often, culture change is not merely desirable but indeed vital for survival.

It is now time to consider some of the practical difficulties experienced by organizations on the fraught journey to corporate culture change.

PART II

THE METHODOLOGY OF CHANGE

❖

A DEFINITION OF METHODOLOGY

We live in a world where certain words are becoming debased through too frequent and imprecise usage. Take strategy and tactics, for instance. Graduates of military academies have for decades been familiar with the general nature of strategy (for instance, how we plan to conduct this campaign) as opposed to the specific nature of tactics (for instance, how this ruse will expose our enemy's flanks).

Strategy has, of course, slipped into the business world and thence into general parlance. Tactics has not. The result is that one minute we talk about the strategy for turnaround at Bloggs Enterprises and the next minute we talk about our strategy for talking to the employees. The first is strategy; the second is tactics.

Does this matter? I think it does. By using one word for both meanings, both meanings are weakened. Lose a word and you lose a concept. Dangerous. Personally, I do not want my welfare to be in pawn to a general who doesn't understand the difference between strategy and tactics.

So it is with methodology and method. Method is how we do something. We tie ourselves on to our climbing rope with a figure-of-eight knot, perhaps a bowline, but never with a granny knot. In other words, we use an appropriate method. In management, however, we don't use the word method any more. (Why use a short word, when you can use a longer one?) Method, like tactics, is falling into obsolescence and we now call it **methodology**.

We say, for example, 'This is our chosen methodology for interpersonal change....' Sorry. We've just had a mega-reading on the bullshit detector. I think you mean your chosen method for interpersonal change. Don't you? Yes, I thought so.

Some people use methodology to mean a collection of methods, for instance the fabled consultant's methodology which turns out to be their favourite toolkit. This is still not good enough.

Method is how we do something. **Methodology** is why we do it that way, i.e. according to that method. If we don't know why we're using a method, then heaven help us.

This part of the book is called 'The Methodology of Change', because it deals with people's concepts about change, typically the concepts which they have as they embark upon a change process. Part II thus relates to the beginning of the change cycle, as distinct from Part III which deals with the later implementation phase of the change cycle.

Most industrial projects, for instance construction projects, appear to fail in the middle or later stages when costs overrun and penalties ensue. Nearly always, the projects were wrong at or before the beginning. People knew in their hearts that the project could not be completed on time or to cost, but they were too frightened to speak out.

Most change programmes fail before they ever begin. They fail because people conceptualize about them in an inappropriate manner. When it comes to change most people operate from a condition of pure ignorance. They may say, 'I know my business, therefore I know how to change it.' But they don't.

So please take these case studies to heart. They involve common mistakes which can easily be avoided by taking a little more care, making a little more effort, having a little more patience. Correct these mistakes at the beginning and there will be little cost or inconvenience. Correct them later on and there will be massive cost and inconvenience. Fail to correct them at all and you will fail to change. Enjoy them!

'We're getting ready to get ready...'

❖

'Hmm.... We really should be doing something about ourselves,' Charles Spreadborough murmured, absentmindedly tapping the ebony boardroom table with his gold pencil. 'I, I'm sorry', David Stevenson, his company secretary replied. 'I'm the one who should be sorry,' Charles apologized. 'Let me be more clear.'

'We keep reading about change...,' Charles indicated his neatly folded copy of *The Financial Times*, 'JIT, MRPII, OPT, the latest methods. And what are we doing at Simulator? Much the same as we've always done.' 'We're making money,' David dourly pointed out. 'That I agree,' retorted Charles, 'But, for all we know, we could be making a great deal more.' 'I suppose so,' David dutifully agreed.

'So what have you got in mind?' asked David, aware that his chairman would, almost certainly, have decided upon something. 'I'm not sure.' Charles ran the tip of his gold pencil across perfect incisors. 'Some sort of independent review, perhaps. Why don't you have a chat with those consultant chappies and

see what they've got to offer?'

After conferring with colleagues and business acquaintances, David obediently drew up a shortlist of six consultancies. Contact was made, meetings were arranged. Five of them stressed their own specialisms. Two offered to write independent reviews for fixed sums. One emphasized the advantages of its 'synchronous manufacturing' package. One offered to put the managers through a series of psychometric tests and another suggested a teambuilding exercise, involving abseiling in the Lake District.

The sixth consultant was different. Unlike the others, he arrived empty-handed. David, expecting yet another glitzy presentation, was nonplussed.

They sat opposite each other in David's office, engaged in ritual small talk for a couple of minutes and sipped David's excellent Brazilian coffee. 'So then, David, what exactly can I do for you?' 'I, I rather thought you would tell me that.' The consultant spread his hands. 'How can I? I don't know what you want.' 'But what does your consultancy do?' 'We help our clients with problems and opportunities. To do that, we need to know them.' Appalled by the reasonableness of this argument, David miserably reflected that he had received no such mandate from Charles.

'The chap did have a point,' David emphasized afterwards. 'Hmm... sounds like bloody cheek to me,' sniffed Charles.

'Anyway, I'm not quite sure it's the right time to be going into this type of consultancy exercise,' he continued, as though he'd never mentioned it in the first place.

Six months later, when Charles again referred to 'a review of some type', David was noticeably unenthusiastic. 'One does need to keep an independent mind, you know,' Charles chided him.

DISCUSSION

Well, this one will run and run.... There will always be the indulgence of wanting 'some kind of review' and there will always be excellent reasons for postponing it. There will always be something else happening. The time will never be quite right.

What does Charles really want? The reassurance of someone from outside telling him that he's doing a good job? An analysis of problems in his company? A political stick to wield? Who knows? Does he? Certainly David is unsure of Charles's real intentions. So how can he assess the consultants and against which needs?

Perhaps unsurprisingly, this is a common syndrome, known to the cognoscenti as 'We're getting ready to get ready.' It merely results in wasted time and worsening relationships. Charles's credibility has suffered; David is correspondingly demotivated. And what do the consultants think about David? They are unlikely to be impressed by his unprofessionalism.

All this is sad. As David says, they are making money, and, as Charles rightly notes, perhaps they could be making much more.

Charles's indecision may be due to not knowing what he wants. If, however, as David suspects, Charles has already reached conclusions, then on what basis? They are almost certain to be premature. Perhaps Charles needs to grow up enough to stop acting the part of the all-knowing company chairman and be honest with David. They are doing well; might they do better? What could help them? By all means, talk to several people; but let's have the decency and professionalism not to waste their time.

What do Charles and David feel they have learned so far? Will independent reviews really help their business, or, more likely, will they gather dust in a filing cabinet? How much will psychometrics and/or teambuilding add to the bottom line and by when? (And what guarantees are there?) What exactly is 'synchronous manufacturing' and what has it achieved to date? Why do the respective consultants feel that their approaches are relevant?

The sixth consultant is undoubtedly the most promising. No bullshit here, no glitzy presentation – just empty hands, an alert mind and a straightforward manner. Utter commonsense. David and Charles don't know what they want of a consultant, which is fair enough. Therefore a responsible consultant must educate them.

At this stage, consultancy needs to be professionally, not commercially, driven. Consultants should be true professionals, not salespeople in disguise. Ironically, initial client meetings, before any paid work has been undertaken, are often the most skill-intensive part of the consulting cycle. Get this part wrong and everything downstream will also be wrong. *Caveat emptor*.

KEY POINTS

- Often people contemplating change do not know what they want.
- Even when problems have been defined, such definition may be incomplete, if not incorrect.
- A good consultant will help a prospective client define problems and develop reasonable expectations.
- Eliciting true client needs, as distinct from stated ones, can be surprisingly difficult.
- A good consultant should be knowledgeable about methodology, not just method.
- 'Getting ready to get ready' is unprofessional. It is also a personal defence against change. It says 'I'm a joker, I'm not serious.'

PRINCIPLE

Procrastination is a waste of everyone's time.

'Just stirring things up...'

❖

Aubrey Lambert's appointment as vice-chancellor was greeted with more than a little dismay in some quarters. 'Bloody man,' snapped Miriam Quentin of the English faculty, 'what in heaven's name does he know about running a university? And a Philistine to boot. His work on the commission was scarcely distinguished, I might add.'

'Now, now, Miriam,' her colleague, Jocelyn Peabody, mildly rebuked. 'Let's give the poor chap the benefit of the doubt. We'll find out soon enough what he's made of.' 'Really, Jocelyn, you can be most insufferably tolerant at times,' retorted Miriam. 'I am reliably assured that he is indeed odious.'

Each morning, Aubrey arrived at half past six in his gleaming black Jaguar. His penchant for sharp suits and knife-edge creases was in marked contrast to his colleagues. Grey, immaculately groomed locks were swept up in a distinguished coiffure 'like Tarzan's uncle', as someone irreverently had it.

Aubrey had arrived, as he put it, on a platform for change. 'I'm not an academic like you chaps,' he was fond of saying, to covert groans from men and barely concealed disdain from women. 'But I do know how to run things. And we need to run this place like a business. We must learn the virtues of the private sector.'

'But he's never worked in the private sector,' Nigel Baslow pointed out to no one in particular.

Aubrey had, as he put it, a sharp stick with which he liked to poke. 'That's the way to get change,' he confided to his wife. 'Poke the buggers a bit.' 'Yes dear,' she absentmindedly agreed, more intent on pruning the roses than listening to Aubrey's rhetoric.

Others were less phlegmatic. Chris Evans put the case thus. 'Aubrey's trying to turn this place into a provider of services in the marketplace. But that's not what we're about. I probably bring in more money from outside than anyone else in the university. But that's incidental. It doesn't bother me in the least that Miriam and her chums in the English faculty bring in nothing. So be it. I've worked in private industry before and if

40

that's what I wanted I'd go back to it. But it's not what I want. I want to belong to a university which isn't aping a training company. And while we're at it, would somebody please tell Aubrey that the private sector isn't exactly the shining bastion of efficiency that he seems to think.'

Sadly, nobody did tell Aubrey. And, ironically, it was left to a prominent local businessman to suggest that Aubrey tone down his approach. 'Tone it down!' Aubrey protested. 'But I'm just getting going. Just stirring things up. That's the way to get these chaps to change!' No, it isn't, he was told bluntly.

DISCUSSION

Aubrey's confidante is right. What he is doing is entirely irresponsible and unprofessional. He is prodding and poking in an effort to initiate change. But he doesn't know what change is required or how to achieve it. He is causing only damage.

Clearly there was prejudice towards Aubrey before he arrived. A few people were prepared to give him a fair hearing; most people probably were not. Aubrey needed to bring debates out into the open, not force his biases against their prejudices. So far his actions have merely resulted in his being viewed as a particularly crass culture attacker opposed by patriotic culture defenders. Currently, both academic standing and fee income are at risk. The departure of Chris Evans, for instance, would sharply diminish both. The irony here is that Aubrey mistakenly views Chris as the exemplar of his new academic.

What is at stake is, of course, the mission of the university. Is it merely a state-assisted provider of services in competition with private sector training bodies? If so, then why accept state funding at all? Alternatively, if it has a separate mission, then what is to be gained in aping the private sector? In fact, why ape any outside agency? Doesn't the university have to ape what it wants to become?

Change is probably necessary. And change may well be painful to colleagues of Chris who have led somewhat cloistered lives. But until mission, strategy and objectives are mapped out, there will be no rationale for change. Unless such mapping is an outcome of free debate, there will be no ownership of change. No marks for Aubrey thus far!

KEY POINTS

O   Seeking to provoke change is unprofessional, irresponsible and counterproductive.

O   For any organization, mission, strategy, objectives and corresponding gaps to be crossed will provide a clear rationale for change, where necessary.

O   The greater the degree of people's involvement in creating and managing change, the greater the resulting ownership of such change.

○   Embarking upon change without an understanding of methodology is akin to playing Russian roulette.

PRINCIPLE

Seeking to provoke change is unprofessional, irresponsible and counterproductive.

'We bought the dream...'

❖

Robin Farmer, the managing director of Capella Electronics, was a man of intelligence, purpose and vision. He wanted the best for his company, his people and himself. Usually he got it.

At a conference on corporate strategy, Robin first came across the concept of Total Quality Management (TQM). Instantly he liked the sound of it. Here was a chance to do things 'right first time', save money in the process and make his company more competitive in the marketplace. All at the same time.

In the months following the conference, Robin learned about TQM. He talked with people, attended conferences and seminars, read books and watched videos. Running his company as managing director was already a full-time job – and more. Learning about TQM at the same time was demanding, to say the least, but he was exhilarated. 'It was fun.'

When Robin felt that he 'knew what he was talking about', he took his board of directors off-site to a country hotel, for a weekend. There they reviewed the principles of TQM, related them to their own company, and 'thrashed out the bare bones of a TQM project', as Robin succinctly put it.

Considerable emphasis was placed upon initial presentations to all levels of the company. Robin insisted upon being personally involved in nearly all of these. After a demanding and punishing schedule, much of the initial doubt and cynicism seemed to have been dispelled. People were 'all fired up and raring to go'.

Six months later, a different picture emerged. When Robin and his board met again at the country hotel, a tale was told of high promise – but poor delivery. 'After that brilliant start-up, we never really got going,' remarked one director, older and wiser from the experience. 'That's right,' a colleague sadly concurred, 'we bought the dream.'

Worse, it now seemed that the board itself had developed grave doubts about TQM. Credibility within the rest of the company, they agreed, was distinctly lacking. Robin, whose brainchild it had been, was aggrieved. When the decision was made to shelve the project, he was personally affronted.

DISCUSSION

Robin and his board did indeed 'buy the dream'. Reality, as always, turns out differently. Robin's initial enthusiasm was admirable – although it might have been better to have involved other people from the beginning, rather than being regarded as 'the TQM expert'.

Capella's main error, however, occurred in the initial weekend session. In making their decision to adopt TQM as the way forward, the directors signed on for a journey without stopping to consider where they were or where they wanted to be. The rhetoric about the journey probably helped to obscure its difficulty.

A better start might have been for Capella to review where it was – in terms of people, operations, marketplace, financial standing, etc. The next step would have been to determine where they wanted to be, why and by when. Such objectives would have acted as imperatives for change. They might well have highlighted the need for new organization – not necessarily different people but, more likely, different methods. TQM could then have been considered as a possible vehicle for progress – and evaluated in terms of its probability in helping them to achieve their objectives.

Great care should have been taken to solicit a wide range of opinion and to reach genuine consensus only after all dissenting views had been thoroughly aired. This would have brought inevitable conflict out in the open where it could be dealt with responsibly. Useful points would have emerged, the possibility of backsliding would have reduced and the whole project would have stood on a much firmer footing.

KEY POINTS

○   A change process is a journey.
○   Before you set out on that journey, you must:
     know where you are.
     know what your objectives are, i.e.
          know where you want to be – and why,
          know how you want to get there,
          know when you expect to get there.
○   Question whether the change programme is realistic in terms of its objectives.

PRINCIPLE

Change objectives must be realistic.

'It's divergent...'

❖

'Well, girl, I'd say we're off to a good start!' Stella Stevens grinned, looking around with satisfaction at the empty auditorium. 'Two hundred people per presentation – and not a yawn from any of 'em. Gripping stuff.' She laughed, self-consciously. 'Even though I say so myself. Come on Sally, let's get back to my office for a celebratory drink.' Sally James, small, Welsh and as dark as Stella was vividly fair, pushed through the swing doors beside her friend and boss. Stella's lavish office was naturally situated on the seventh floor – the executive suite. 'Stella Stevens, Group Human Resources Director' was triumphantly emblazoned on the door.

Inside, they kicked off their shoes and raised two glasses of Laphroaig. 'Well, kid, stick with me,' Stella laughed. 'The Electricity Supply Industry is over-ripe for change.' She squinted at the huge photograph of a hydroelectric scheme in the Highlands which took pride of place on the wall opposite her desk. 'And we're the ones to give 'em it.'

Sally sipped her whisky thoughtfully. When she spoke, she chose her words carefully, tentatively voicing a concern which had nagged away at her during the preceding days. 'Stella, I fully agree with what you say about change. And I do feel that the HR Department has a key role to play. By the end of the week, we'll have got our message across to nearly a thousand people.' She paused. Stella looked at her narrowly, expectantly.

'I just wonder whether we're going about things in the right way.' 'The right way?' Stella queried menacingly. 'Well, it is all a bit ... a bit divergent, isn't it?' Sally nervously suggested.

'Divergent? What do you mean – divergent?' Stella pounced, dramatically arching pencilled eyebrows.

'Well ... at the moment, I can't see any focus. I mean, what will people actually do – after they've been to the seminars?' 'Do? Do? There will be plenty for them to do. I can promise you that,' retorted Stella. 'Yes, but what?' Sally doggedly persisted.

DISCUSSION

This change programme is indeed divergent. It will run and run – until it runs out of steam. At this point, someone will publicly note that results seem to be conspicuous by their absence. The change programme will then become utterly discredited and will consequently be abandoned. The next person who tries to effect change will have an even harder struggle.

All of which would be a great pity – and all of which is avoidable. Sally's comments are entirely fair. One cannot believe that the creators of the pyramids said to themselves, 'Let's go off into the desert and build something.' And yet this is exactly what Stella is contemplating. The Ancient Egyptians knew exactly what they were doing; so must she and so must the entire executive leadership.

It is vital that change derives from business objectives and is driven by top management. The human resources role should best be facilitative. It is complementary to but no substitute for line management ownership.

Change is a journey, a series of destinations, each one a staging post for the next. It is vital to focus upon reaching these staging posts.

Stella's educational seminars are an excellent beginning, but that is all they are – a beginning. After that, change must go from macro (industry/corporate) level to micro (business unit/individual) level. Managers of operating businesses must be helped to conceive what change means for their businesses in terms of specific processes and outcomes. The key word is 'specific'. Without focus upon specifics, benefits will not be realized. The real effort is yet to come.

KEY POINTS

○   Change is a journey, a series of destinations; each destination is a staging post for the next.
○   Change programmes usually need to be initially divergent, to encompass all of the people and their concerns.
○   Equally, however, change programmes must become focused on particular destinations, stated outcomes.
○   Change must ultimately focus on improved results.

PRINCIPLE

Change must ultimately focus on improved results.

'It's going to be top-down..."

❖

'The Plexity Corporation is large, respectable, diversified – and dull,' began Gerald, the bright young thing from corporate affairs. 'It also pays my salary,' he rather lamely added, gazing in startled dismay from his fellow delegates to the singularly unamused group of senior executives sitting opposite.

Too late, Gerald realized the true value of this 'outstanding career opportunity', which had, seemingly unaccountably, come his way. Several of his companions from the Strategy Unit fervently hoped that the heat would stay off them. Too bad if Gerry fried in the hot seat. It couldn't happen to a better guy.

Lacking any alternative, Gerald irresolutely continued – continued to explain that the previous era's diversification strategy had been 'fine for its time, but times have changed. There are global sociopolitical and macroeconomic factors which threaten our core businesses – spread even as they are across different industries.' And, with a wealth of facts and figures, graphs and charts, young Gerald proceeded to explain just what these factors were and how Plexity would be affected.

Essentially, Gerald's argument was simple. Plexity had to change fast. That meant an RDP (Radical Development Programme to the uninitiated). Headquarters had to get 'all those businesses out there to shape up – or ship out', Gerald emphasized, unwisely.

The heads of the operating divisions looked across at their HQ compatriots in disdain. Finally one spoke.

'Gerald,' he said, in a tone which implied that such familiarity was a disease. 'This change programme which you're talking about ...' He held up a weary hand as Gerald started to mouth 'R ...' 'Yeah, I know, I know ... RIP – wasn't it?'

He waited until the nervous laughter had died down before turning once more to a discomfited Gerald.

'Anyway,' he continued, 'this change programme.... Tell me something,' he asked with exquisite innocence, 'is it going to be top-down or bottom-up?' 'Oh, top-down, definitely,' beamed Gerald.

DISCUSSION

Plexity needs to stop right here. This plan will never work. Never!

So what is wrong? Just about everything. Gerald will assuredly have done his homework thoroughly (although has anyone bothered to check on some of the assumptions behind those impressive graphs and curves?). Gerald may well be right. Plexity probably does need to change – and fast.

But HQ-led? Not over our dead bodies, say the operational heads. What do the bright boys at head office know about our businesses? Could they run them? (Could they fly to the moon?) So why try to tell us? And that promise to ship out? Just you wait and see who ends up being shipped out.

Top-down here means that those at, or near, the top cannot see all the way down the management structure to the remote underworlds where people make profits, some of which help support head office. And head office, ironically enough, actually does have some good ideas, if only they were properly implemented.

But the RDP will not be properly implemented. Already it's lost credibility with senior managers. (What chance has it got, lower down, if they don't believe in it?) And that RIP tag won't go away. Already politics is obscuring the issues – issues which may well be critical for Plexity's survival.

To escape from the impending morass, action needs to be taken now. Let's get those operating managers together jointly to review the business – which is their business. Let's have a moratorium on solutions, even (especially!) RDP, until issues have been aired and problems defined. Then let's get the operating managers to devise a change programme that is relevant to their needs, one of which they can take ownership and to which they can be committed. And let's get them, in turn, to check their people's reactions. More care at the beginning means less chaos later on.

KEY POINTS

○   If change is simply top-down, it never reaches the bottom.
○   'The bottom' of a management structure is the only place where operations happen and profits are made.
○   Top-down change, on its own, is, therefore, inadequate.
○   Change may have started top-down. To have any chance of success, it needs quickly to become both top-down and bottom-up.

PRINCIPLE

Change needs to be both top-down and bottom-up.

'It's bottom-up...'

❖

Briggs and Titterton was a heavy engineering company, based in Yorkshire. 'Where there's muck, there's brass' was an oft-quoted sentiment in that part of the world; it was certainly true enough at Briggs, where both were to be had in abundance.

As a traditional industry in a traditional setting, Briggs had been slow to adopt quality circles and what few had started up quickly perished – all, that is, except for that run by Jimmy McKenzie.

Jimmy McKenzie was a giant of a man, 'big and bull-necked as me mam used to say'. His family had worked at Briggs for three generations. Jimmy was a fitter. His obvious intelligence and his easy way with people had, early on, marked him out as a man 'with management potential'. But Jimmy preferred to stay where he was – on the tools. 'I know my place,' he was fond of saying, 'and it's not with them upstairs.'

However, Jimmy McKenzie's quality circle attracted the attention of 'them upstairs' by its seeming ability to resolve pressing problems quickly. 'I must say, that chap McKenzie certainly seems to get results,' commented Horace Sykes, the Group MD, on a rare visit to the Briggs and Titterton works, near Wakefield.

'McKenzie?' queried George Kelly, the Works Manager. 'I didn't know you knew him.' 'Know him? Of course I know him,' scoffed Sykes. 'Knew his father before him. Fine fellow, fine fellow.'

Emboldened by this show of approval, some of the other quality circle members suggested taking on more ambitious projects. 'What about changing the stores system?' Stan Unwin suggested. 'Aye, and reorganizing those galoots in sales', chipped in Graham Owen. Only Jimmy remained unconvinced. 'Them upstairs mightn't like it,' he said. Nor would he be dissuaded from this outlook.

DISCUSSION

Jimmy is right. 'Them upstairs' might not indeed like some of the more radical suggestions spawned by the quality circle. Worse, they might feel that their own functions were being usurped. Worse still, they might decide that their own jobs were on the line. Already Kelly may be in danger of emerging as an enemy of change – any change.

Many quality circles encounter this problem. Flushed with a few well-deserved triumphs, they try for something bigger, only to find that they bump hard against an invisible glass ceiling. Success at an operational level practically always guarantees failure at an organizational level. People wrongly assume that skills at an operational level (analysis/relatively simple implementation) are the same as the skills required at an organizational level (political sensitivity, communication, influencing, negotiation).

Top-down and bottom-up change strategies both run into a common problem – the organization. It exists between top management and the shop floor. Often its primary function seems to be to play off one against the other. It is a labyrinth of vested interest. The organization – typically middle management – can easily feel itself squeezed from both sides. Its natural response is to filter out bottom-up change and hopelessly dilute top-down change.

For change to succeed, the organization needs to be actively involved. Jimmy's quality circle is never going to sort out the stores system or the sales department by itself. It needs help from above to translate ideas into action and ensure that 'them upstairs' have genuine ownership of change. What about the people in stores and sales? Without active involvement, they too will vigorously fight any changes imposed on them by Jimmy's quality circle, or anyone else for that matter.

KEY POINTS

○   If change initiatives are merely bottom-up, they never reach the top, so they lack power and die.

○   Change must be bottom-up, (empowering the people who get results) and top-down (top management ensuring that such empowering actually takes place).

○   It's important to avoid parts of the organization being viewed as winners while others are viewed as losers. 'Winners and losers' scenarios are to nobody's ultimate advantage.

PRINCIPLE

Change needs to be both bottom-up and top-down.

'We need an attitude change around here!'

❖

'Attitude! It all comes down to one word. Attitude! The right attitude.' Sarah Forward stared grimly at Richard Harrison, the managing director of Gardyloo Enterprises. 'And your people haven't got it.' Harrison paled before the new owner. 'I wouldn't quite say that,' he weakly protested. 'Well I would,' snapped Forward.

'I phoned up yesterday, posing as an irate customer,' Forward continued. 'Twelve rings on the switchboard to get through. It should have been not more than four.' 'That's unusual,' Harrison weakly explained. 'It must have been a busy period.' 'It was lunchtime,' Forward brutally retorted. 'But, just to give the benefit of the doubt, I tried again later on. Same result.' Harrison sagged wearily in defeat.

'I was put through to after-sales, then sales, then "someone in the factory". Nobody gave me their name or title.

Nobody accepted responsibility for my problem. And nobody fixed it.' She fixed Harrison with a level stare. 'Nobody was the least bit bothered!'

'That's unfair.' Harrison practically wailed. 'They do care.' 'Do they?' Forward remorselessly continued. 'Then why did the girl in the sales office say, "I'm absolutely fed up taking these bloody customer complaints! Nobody seems to know what the hell they're doing in this place."'

Silence. Harrison slumped in utter misery. 'She's new here. A stand-in for Sandra.' 'Forget her,' Forward brusquely told him. 'She's history!'

She leaned back and spoke with slow deliberation. 'Your people haven't got the right attitude. And, believe me, they're going to have it. I've got a psychologist flying in from California.' She glanced pointedly at her watch. 'She should be with us in about two hours.'

DISCUSSION

The problems have, to some degree, already been stated. In two hours, with the arrival of the fabled psychologist from California, they may well worsen.

Forward's criticism of Gardyloo's after-sales service certainly needs investigating. Did she pick a particularly bad day or is this truly the norm? Further investigation is required. Even if she did pick a particularly bad day, is Gardyloo happy with such an appalling level of service? Can it afford to be? For how long will its customers accept such indifference before looking elsewhere?

Focusing upon after-sales service, however, may be a mistake. There may be other, more critical areas of the company which are more deserving of urgent attention. Attitudinal problems in one department are frequently duplicated in others, because they usually derive from a company-wide culture. If this is the case here, the problems at Gardyloo are company-wide.

Concentrating solely on attitude, while tempting, is emphatically not the answer. When you criticize someone's attitude, you immediately invite resistance. Our attitudes are too close to our psyche, our personal culture of identity and belief, to be altered without a considerable struggle.

Again the assumption is that to change behaviour and results, you first have to change attitude. Nothing could be further from the truth. In order to change attitude you first have to change behaviour and results. At Gardyloo, people need to realize the consequences of their behaviour. Equally, management needs to realize the reasons behind such behaviour. Sarah needs to stop acting like a tyrant (a behavioural change in itself) and start to help people to change their behaviour. She will rapidly find that people are far more willing to change behaviour than attitude – it's far less threatening.

The after-sales service section needs re-education, development and training. Probably so do many other parts of the company. A company-wide change programme should be considered.

KEY POINTS

○   Trying to change people's attitudes is likely to be perceived as highly threatening. People will resist.

○   Changing attitude will not change behaviour and results, because changing attitude will not work. But changing behaviour and results will change attitude.

○   Attitude thus changed will lock into place new behaviour and results.

PRINCIPLE

Trying to change behaviour by changing attitude is approaching the problem from the wrong direction. It will fail.

'One hell of a culture problem...'

❖

'These guys have one hell of a culture problem.' Sam Fulton, the recently appointed general manager of Zeta Communications, hitched his trousers above a spreading waistline and turned to Scott Winrow, his young assistant. 'They're engineers, not managers. They seem to think that we're running a state of the art engineering company. We should be running a state of the art business company.' 'Yes, sir,' the Harvard-trained Winrow dutifully murmured.

'Just look at these figures.' Fulton threw away the wad of computer printout in disgust. 'There's no cost control, no daily management information. It's service at any price – and damn the expense! The result? For the last three quarters, our operating profit has been dipping. Two more months of that and we'll be running at a loss.' Fulton's outstretched forefinger stabbed the air. 'Scott, I'll be damned if I let that happen.' 'No sir,' Winrow agreed.

Further discussion followed. The more he considered it, the more certain Fulton felt. The culture was all wrong. Good, old-fashioned tight financial control, that was the answer. Get these engineers filling out proper requisitions, not just scribbling what they liked on pieces of paper. That way, the spend could be scrutinized. Scrutinized and evaluated.

But first, he'd have to spend some money himself. Fulton frowned as he drove home that evening. Management accountants would have be recruited, and systems people. But with proper controls in place.... He resisted the temptation to rub his hands gleefully.

Next morning, Fulton rang straight through to Burgess in human relations. By midday, the first recruitment advertisement had been placed.

DISCUSSION

Fulton is setting himself up for failure. Worse, he is unwittingly setting up the whole of Zeta for failure. Yes, it is engineering-run, and yes, it lacks business discipline, but Fulton's move to improve discipline via systems/financial control will be widely viewed as an attack on the existing culture.

When people are attacked, or when they think they are being attacked, they defend. They defend by attacking, in turn, those whom they consider to be their enemies. In this case, the engineers of Zeta don't have far to look. Those accountants and systems people? Right first time!

The scene is thus set for tribal war. The 'old guard' will quite sincerely believe that 'We're engineers and we're proud of it. Engineering is what made this company what it is' and the 'new guard' will claim 'These people must become businessmen first and engineers second.' Before long, stereoptypes will have formed. 'We're loyal to Zeta, we've worked here for years. These new people, with their inflated salaries. Who are they loyal to? How long will they be here for?'

The way to avoid this war is not to enter it in the first place. Fulton needs to share the problem with the only people who can ultimately resolve it. Fulton must go out and talk with people along the lines of, 'Sure Zeta has superlative engineering skills. But it's also rapidly becoming unprofitable. Doubtless there are sound operational reasons for our rising costs. But unless costs are curbed or revenues increase, sooner or later, all of us will be out of a job.'

Fulton wants to change results. He thinks that changing culture is the best way to change results. He's wrong. He needs to trust his operations staff with his problem – their problem. He needs to work with them to enable them to make changes in their behaviour which will produce long-term results. If outside specialists are needed (and they probably will be), they must be carefully brought into the company and equally carefully integrated within it.

KEY POINTS

○   Trying directly to change culture is even more futile than trying directly to change attitudes.

○   The existing culture must first be understood. The implicit must be made explicit. This is a delicate process best performed by skilled outsiders.

○   Inevitably the existing culture will have productive and counterproductive aspects. People need to understand them.

○   Great care must be taken to avoid a culture 'attackers and defenders' syndrome.

○   People must understand how culture is formed, why it exists, what tend to be the good and bad aspects and why focusing on behaviour and results is more apt to succeed.

PRINCIPLE

Trying to change behaviour by changing culture is approaching the problem from the wrong direction. It will fail.

'We got the package'

❖

Colin Lawson, the chief executive of Sigma Joinery Products, was a worried man. He should, he reflected wryly, be a happy one. His company had a sound reputation, an excellent product range and a full order book. It also seemed to have developed a chronic inability to meet those orders. To put it bluntly, product never seemed to stay off the factory floor long enough to get out the door.

Inevitably, accusing fingers had long been pointed, particularly in the direction of Jim Armitage, Colin's production director. As the relevant functional director, he was directly accountable for production output. Colin sighed. Jim was, in his book, a good chap who tried hard. The problem was that trying hard just didn't seem to be enough.

Something had to be done – and quickly. Colin talked with several outside sources and was recommended the P>I>R> – F! system. Apparently this strange acronym stood for Put It Right – Fast! which, after all, was exactly what Colin wanted. Developed several years previously in

Detroit, it had, in the words of one devotee, 'worked miracles in a number of leading companies'.

P>I>R> – F! was a production package applicable to a wide range of industries. It involved a rigid discipline in following a highly specialized network of systems and procedures. Used properly, the designers promised it would transform an entire production area.

It did. In the caustic words of Jim Armitage, P>I>R> – F! transformed his production department from 'an admitted limbo into an unmitigated hell', Paperwork doubled overnight – and then trebled – to everyone's dismay. Production output dipped and dipped again. It soon became tacitly acknowledged that, to get anything at all out the door, you had 'to do things the old way'. Thus production managers were forced into the untenable position of propagating and defending a system which they personally by-passed.

Relationships between the production department and other departments in Sigma had never been warm. Now they became positively glacial. The sales department, in particular, alternately jeered and wailed.

Colin viewed the entire fiasco with (he thought) well-justified wrath. Not only had the P>I>R> – F! package not improved the situation, it had actually made it much worse. Public outrage had to be suitably appeased. It was with a heavy heart that he took the decision to 'let Jim Armitage go'.

DISCUSSION

Colin bought a solution to a problem. He felt that he had defined the problem well enough – 'lack of production output'. His saviour, the P>I>R> – F! package, promised to give him a ready solution which, unfortunately, didn't work.

A package is a solution. Furthermore, it is a solution which is deemed to have wide applicability. The plain truth is that 'big' management problems, such as 'lack of production output' are rarely susceptible to packaged solutions – whatever their purveyors claim. Indeed, the notion that one can develop solutions into which people's problems will somehow neatly fit, is strikingly naive.

Colin needed to understand the problem and, perhaps more importantly, enable other people to understand it also. He knew that there was a lack of production output; he didn't, however, know why that lack of production output existed.

Often the best way to investigate a problem is to treat the problem as a symptom of a deeper problem, which may itself be a symptom of yet deeper problems. In this way, 'big' management problems, when correctly diagnosed, will usually be found to have a shockingly complex hierarchy of causes. While such diagnosis may be formidable, the hard part is yet to come. Which causes should be tackled in which order (and how, and why) to resolve the original problem once and for all?

KEY POINTS

○   Packages are solutions waiting for problems. With important management problems, this approach rarely works.

○   Start with the problem. Correctly define it. Then regard the problem as a symptom. Treat it as the tip of an iceberg.

○   Define the network of causes of the problem, i.e. the main body of the iceberg. Then decide which causes to tackle first and how to tackle them.

○   A package cannot do your thinking for you. Don't expect it to. Do your own thinking – you are the one who will have to live with the results.

PRINCIPLE

Packaged solutions don't work.

'We've tried it...'

❖

The Alpha Design Company was 'a traditional firm run on traditional lines', according to Jim Cooper, the managing director and nephew of the founder. Indeed, on that grim April morning in 1947 when Eddie Cooper had been demobbed into a harshly opportunistic post-war world, who could have forseen that he would one day turn Alpha into the foremost design company outside London?

Eddie had nous, some accountancy training interrupted by the war, and contacts in the most surprising places. He also had a tidy stake of highly personal income from his efforts in running the sergeants' mess while simultaneously supplying liquor to local GIs. Eddie's assets – nous, accountancy, contacts and easy money – stood him in good stead in the years to come.

And the years to come were good to Eddie. In the fifties and sixties, Alpha went from strength to strength. As Eddie said, 'What do I know about design? Not a lot. But I do know about running a company. And Alpha's a traditional company run on traditional lines.'

Being traditional, though, wasn't such a good recipe for success in the seventies and eighties. One thing you could always say for Eddie, he knew when to get in and he knew when to get out. By the time he retired to the Formentor peninsula and Jim took over the company, it was 'a right mess and make no mistake'.

Fixing the mess proved elusive and Alpha had several false starts, 'several little flirtations with outside people'. O & M didn't work, MIS didn't work, TQ didn't work. 'You mention it,' Jim laughed wryly, 'and if it's got an initial, we've tried it. No bloody use, none of 'em.

'Finally we came across this chap from the local university. Professor of Organization Development, he called himself. We told him about all these different approaches which hadn't worked and he said, "That's right. They won't work. They can't work. The problem's your culture. It's rejecting solutions like a body rejects a heart transplant." So I suggested, "Come along then and give us something that won't be

59

rejected" and he said, "I'll come along and help you not to reject things in the first place."

'Well, fair enough, but it goes on and on. You've got to give this chap his due, he does talk a good fight. But seminars on this, sessions on that ... we're doing workshops next, like they do at Art College. We never stop talking. Talking about this, talking about that. How we feel about ourselves, about Alpha being a family company, even how we feel about old Eddie, who's probably laughing his socks off by now. Mufti flufti's all very well but I've got a business to run. When we got into this, we didn't think it would take so much effort. If words were pound notes, we'd all be rich men!'

DISCUSSION

Alpha is a typical pioneer organization (as described in Part I), imbued with Eddie's personal philosophies. It is not 'a traditional firm run on traditional lines'. It is Eddie's firm run on Eddie's lines – even through he is no longer present.

Eddie's way – the pioneer phase – has had its day. It doesn't work any more and consequently the company is suffering because the old culture – Eddie's culture – is still intact. The company needs to develop a form of the systems phase which is right for it.

As our Professor of Organization Development has rightly observed, the problem is primarily cultural. Until this problem is worked through, technical and managerial enhancements, however worthy in their own right, will be wasted.

So – more talk, more effort, and more pain than one might imagine. But our professor must make clear to people why they have to go through such a dark tunnel, what labour is required, and when daylight may reasonably be expected.

Culture change is consuming of time and commitment. Whatever the business reasons behind culture change, it is ultimately about people. It is certainly not susceptible to quick fixes. The only productive way to achieve it is to help people to work through social and political issues (such as, 'Is this the most appropriate style of management?' or 'What happens if we decentralize power?'). Working through such issues may at first seem like management games. In the end, it may grow to seem like the game of life itself. And this game, as we all know, is no easy one. Such progression needs the assistance of a suitably skilled facilitator. Our professor at least belongs to the right discipline. A facilitator, like a therapist, has considerable professional responsibilities. He or she must make clear to all concerned why such a process is being undertaken, what are its costs, benefits and pitfalls, and how long it will reasonably take. It must be understood that the aim of such activities as workshops is not to produce sterile talking shops but rather to create mechanisms for progress. If progress does not occur, and is not seen to occur, the whole process will quickly be discredited.

KEY POINTS

○   Educate yourself about change before you attempt it.
○   Experimenting with change – trying different approaches – is apt to be a costly and destructive indulgence.
○   Get the best help there is. It just might be the best investment you ever make.
○   Don't let a change process ramble. Lock it into a project or a series of projects.
○   Change needs to be organic, but it also needs to be controlled.
○   Change takes five times as much effort as you thought. (The same multiple applies to starting up your own business, so maybe it's best to hang on in there!)

PRINCIPLE

With change, don't try it. Do it.

'We're doing it ourselves...'

❖

'There are no two ways about it,' Nigel Lindsay emphasized. 'We've got to change. And I don't mean a few minor changes here or there. We've got to change our entire culture.' He paused, dramatically surveying the array of rapt faces. 'And what's more, we've got to do it ourselves. Nobody else can do it for us!' He sat down to a roar of applause.

There was ferocious activity during the following months. A steering committee was convened, special task forces were set up, problems were enthusiastically tackled. For a time, there did indeed seem to be the semblance of change.

'But it'll take more than one swallow to change this summer,' drily noted Joe Falstaff, the works convenor. 'Oh, it's not that I doubt Nigel's sincerity, but some-times I wonder whether he realizes that some of his key people aren't really so loyal to the company. They're more what you might call loyal to themselves.'

Sadly Joe's observation proved apt. As summer dwindled into autumn, the pendulum of change which had initially swung widely, began to swing equally widely back again to the status quo. Glass ceilings and glass walls were painfully hit.

'The trouble with this place is that there's too much talk and not enough progress,' said Billy Westgate in production control. 'We're choking on our own politics. It's all very well for Nigel to say that we're the only ones who can change our culture. The plain fact of it is that, on current evidence, we can't.'

DISCUSSION

If culture is 'the set of assumptions implicit in behaviour', then there is an obvious problem for any organization trying to change its culture. If something is implicit then you are unaware of it. If you're unaware of it, how on earth are you going to change it?

Nigel, Joe, Billy and the rest are hopelessly trapped in their own culture. This is in no way their fault. Rather, it's inevitable. Without some kind of common culture their social grouping would not persist. While culture is an invisible social glue which binds them together, it is necessarily as effective in resisting change. This is its great strength – and its great weakness.

In any organization, the corporate culture will be an amalgam of many different cultures, each corresponding to different groups within the company. Each group will have its own power base, its own agenda, its own concerns, and its own definitions of what is and is not important. In short, each group will have its own politics.

Where people are gathered together, politics is inevitable. If you deny this, you are deluding yourself. Politics is the pursuit of power, and power is control over (though not necessarily ownership of) scarce resources. Of all resources, probably the most scarce and consequently the most prized is social meaning.

To some degree people are alike, and to some degree they are different. We are different in that we are of different ages, have different personal histories, have different values and different motivations. These differences lead us to view common situations in different ways. One man's terrorist is another's freedom fighter. Whichever social meaning prevails ('These people are freedom fighters', 'It's all the production department's fault') is of profound political significance. It sets the agenda.

In organizations, the politics of difference entails a struggle for whose meaning shall prevail. In the process, there is the usual finger-pointing and allocating of blame. Sadly, often everyone becomes a victim and the politics usually just gets worse.

One temptation is to have 'an objective outside view' from consultants. Often, when provided, such views are instantly marginalized by comments such as, 'What do they know about our business?' Better by far to invite in a suitably skilled outsider to help people make explicit their subjective views. The next step is to make explicit the assumptions behind such views. At this point, cultural variables start to become strikingly clear. People will say, 'Yes, we always took these things for granted, but now it's as though we're seeing them for the very first time.' Previously invisible barriers (our glass ceilings) will become visible. Like the Berlin Wall, they too may be dismantled when the need for them has gone.

Do companies really need an outside consultant to help with this process? I believe the answer is yes – for several reasons. Insiders are culturally tainted by the very virtue of being insiders. They're bound to be affected by the culture. Insiders are also part of the politics of the company, and, fairly or unfairly, are apt to be distrusted. Few insiders could possibly have the necessary time and fewer still the required skill. Developing culture change is a highly skill-intensive activity, involving many years of theory and practice. If it were easy then almost anyone could succeed. Experience and research suggests that very few people can and do succeed.

So DIY culture change, like DIY brain surgery, isn't to be recommended. What patient would be their own surgeon? What client could be their own therapist? It doesn't work. It can't.

KEY POINTS

○   DIY culture change cannot work.
○   The implicit must be made explicit.
○   Only the explicit may be successfully resolved.
○   Finding the right specialist may prove time-consuming and costly. This is as nothing to the cost of getting it wrong.

PRINCIPLE

DIY culture change doesn't work. It can't.

'We've got these hot-shot consultants'

❖

'Let's face it,' said John Williams, 'culture change is just not going to happen around here. Not', he added significantly, 'if it's left to us, that is.' He looked around him expectantly. There was silence from the assembled multitude. So be it, he thought.

The following week the consultants from Forbes moved in. They positively radiated confidence and expertise. Young and keen, their favourite response was 'Can do!' They had MBAs from the best international business schools. They wore dark, expensive suits with discreet but expensive accessories, and shoes which 'gleamed like Attila the Hun's freshly honed blade', as one wag lyrically put it.

'We must ceaselessly search for the unshakeable facts,' Harold Geneen had memorably said in another place and time. These boys and girls proceeded to emulate his dictum. And how....

Facts and figures ruled supreme. Analysis was king. Profit analysis, cost analysis, overhead analysis, overhead value analysis. 'Every kind of analysis that I've ever heard of,' muttered John Williams, unsure whether to be impressed or depressed. 'And some that I haven't,' he added ruefully.

'Get the facts. Then make the decisions.' That was the multi-media message to generals and troops alike. And never before had so many facts been revealed.

The problem was that, having let the consultants dig up the facts, John's managers seemed equally content to let them make the decisions. 'After all, that's what they're being paid for,' one senior figure remarked. 'Why have a dog and bark yourself?'

DISCUSSION

In this situation, culture change is not only unlikely, it is impossible. The so-called change programme is consultant-driven, with no ownership by the clients. The clients are quite prepared to sit back and let the consultants run the company. The consultants have fallen into the trap. When they inevitably make mistakes in running a business whose technicalities they do not understand, they will become utterly discredited.

Even if, in the short term, better decisions are being made, what will happen when the consultants leave? The present management will be further enfeebled and even more incompetent. Any change will ultimately be counterproductive.

The consultants must stop acting as surrogate managers, employing (illegitimate) authority which the real managers have temporarily abdicated. They are general management consultants, not managers; their job is to help people to help themselves.

Consultancy style must change from an **expert** role (here are the facts and figures, this is what you must do) to a **process** role (we will help you find the best way for you to manage your particular business needs).

The emphasis must shift from the purely rational world of facts and figures to managing a human and therefore messy process of change. Where does the company need to be – and why? How is it going to get there? What resources are available? What barriers will have to be overcome? What skills are needed to overcome them? These are painful questions which painfully need answering.

KEY POINTS

○   General management consultancy is not surrogate or locum management.

○   Consultancy style may be expert or process. With general management problems a process style is usually more appropriate.

○   During a project, the emphasis may swing between expert and process. It is essential, however, that at any time both consultants and clients know which mode is being employed and why.

○   Process consultants may also be good expert consultants, although this is unlikely. Expert consultants almost always make poor process consultants.

○   Consultants helping clients to change their culture must operate primarily in a process mode.

PRINCIPLE

Process consultancy is vital for culture change.

'We've got too much change!'

❖

Frank Stapleton sat opposite Hillary Brooke in the empty boardroom. Weak autumn sunlight shone on to the polished mahogany of the boardroom table. Hillary drummed well-manicured fingernails upon it. Finally he spoke.

'Change ... you chaps are always promising change. Well, I'll tell you about change – what it's meant for this company, what it's meant for me.

'This used to be a great little furniture company. Family-owned. Well, they all were, in those days. It turned out products like this table, products that would last a lifetime and more. Much more.

'You know, of course, what happens to little furniture companies. As time goes on, they swallow up each other. It's a sort of Darwinian impulse. Swallow, or be swallowed. We started off by swallowing, but of course, it couldn't last. Inevitably we were swallowed up by a conglomerate.'

He shrugged. 'Life within a conglomerate isn't all bad. For a start, there was financial muscle. And as long as we produced both cash and profits, they were content to leave us alone. What do they know about furniture-making? All they're interested in making is money.

'For a while, they did make money out of us – and life continued much as before. But in the late eighties, we started to lose our way. It took us a while to recognize it, of course, but the trend was downward. When the recession got under way, our profits dropped like a stone.

'Naturally, at this point, our parents started to get interested. The former MD upped and left. He'd held a considerable share of the equity and made a killing with the sale. He wasn't interested in being under scrutiny. Wise fellow. He was off to his retirement home in Portugal.

'I put in a replacement who lasted six months. He was a big-company man and just couldn't hack an operation that was hands on. After that, the place went for more than a year without an MD. I just couldn't find anyone suitable. In the end, I promoted the production director. He's a good bloke but he's got a fight on his hands. Changes at the top ... the other directors are new as well. Musical chairs.

Understandably, the workforce is pretty confused.

'We've got to get our act right now. The market is desperate. We've got restrictive practices, outdated techniques, no proper production planning and control. Management is weak; in the glory days we could throw money at problems.' He rubbed the mahogany, smiled ruefully. 'Volume covered many sins.

'So, to be honest, the very last thing we need is chaps like you coming along to talk about change. At the moment we don't need more change. Our problem is that we've already got far too much change.'

DISCUSSION

Hillary is viewing change in an entirely inappropriate manner. He sees change as something which is poured into people as water is poured into a jar. At a certain point, people cannot take any more and the jar overflows. He thinks that Frank is coming along to recommend more change which must be sequentially added, thus ensuring overflow.

This view of change is very common and very naive. When expressed, it indicates that people, typically senior managers, don't understand the fundamental meaning of change. If they don't understand change then what hope is there for their staff?

By the sound of it, Hillary's company has succeeded for many years in staving off progress. This was fine as long as someone (the customer) could be persuaded to pay for operational sins. Those days, however, have vanished. The company is left with a severe backlog of problems which have to be resolved. Resolving them seems to have proved a deterrent to at least two managing directors (and how many other senior managers?)

In order for the company to survive, the backlog of changes needs to be resolved in the shortest possible time. The answer does not lie in overloading people; this is simply counterproductive. Nor is the answer to do as Hillary seems to be suggesting and bury one's head in the sand. Naively arranging a series of changes sequentially will not work either; timescales merely expand. Postponing changes until 'some other time' may well ensure that Hillary's company runs out of time.

The time to change is always now. People never change because they want to; they only change because they have to, because a particular threat is confronting them. Already they have delayed; already time is running out.

The trick is to learn about the process of change itself. If you master the ability to change then that ability will stand you in good stead with any change. The more you learn, the shorter the lead time of change and the better the adaptation.

Hillary needs to clear his mind of an outmoded way of thinking. His company has continued for years without necessary change. He has stood by and watched ineptitude follow ineptitude. What will be different this time? He needs to suspend his prejudgement of Frank, pay attention and listen. It may be his last chance.

KEY POINTS

○   Change is not something with which people are passively filled. People are not jars; change is not water.

○   Senior managers need to realize that knowing a business says nothing about their ability to change that business.

○   It's best to approach change as you would approach a serious health problem: obtain the best specialist help you can. It will pay for itself many times over.

○   People's capacity to handle change is potentially infinite. Only a specialist will unlock that potential.

PRINCIPLE

People's capacity to handle change is potentially infinite.

PART III

IMPLEMENTING CHANGE

❖

INTRODUCTION

Broadly speaking, change programmes can be divided into two phases. The first phase is considering change, diagnosing the situation and its resulting needs, and planning what is to happen. Here one needs to go from thinking about change in general to planning for change in particular. As Part II makes clear, this phase is often skimped – with subsequent disastrous results.

The proof of the pudding is, of course, in the eating. Rigorous diagnostics and elegant plans may yet turn out to be irrelevant in that hideous jungle which we laughingly call the real world. Change is ultimately about implementation. With methodology, one is still in the staff college; with implementation, one is on the battlefield.

The following case studies recount experiences on that battlefield. While errors of methodology cost relatively little to correct, errors of implementation cost considerable amounts of time, effort and money to put right. In quality terms, it's the cost of prevention versus the cost of rework.

So enjoy these case studies. Vicarious experience is less powerful than real experience – but it doesn't hurt half as much! Taking heed of these errors of judgement now may help you to avoid them later on. Let's hope so.

'We're traumatized...'

❖

When TCP, the international conglomerate, acquired Vector Chemicals, the general impression among the business community was that they had paid well over the odds. 'A deal too far,' the financial press fulminated. TCP remained undaunted.

'Vector's underperforming in its sector,' Laura March, of TCP, informed her board. 'Sure, we don't know anything about chemicals. But we don't have to. There's lots of knowledge about chemicals in Vector itself. Perhaps too much.' She paused a moment, for maximum effect. 'What we do know about, gentlemen, is management. And what we will bring to Vector is professional management.'

Within days, TCP's financial ferrets had ransacked Vector's business accounts. Ample evidence existed that poor use was being made of fixed assets, the business was too liquid, the age of debt was uncontrolled, working capital was too high. 'We're going to make those assets sweat,' Laura promised. 'You wait and see.'

The first casualties, inevitably, were the directors of Vector who had thoughtfully provided themselves with three-year service contracts. Assessment interviews were then held with all managers, down to and including supervisory level. A third of the managers were deemed unsatisfactory and promptly departed with singularly unlavish compensation. 'One law for them and one for us,' a department head bitterly commented.

The next casualties were the workforce. Personnel levels in indirect areas were reduced by 40 per cent, those in direct areas by 20 per cent. 'And that's just for starters,' one old hand commented. 'This lot will cut and scrape away at fat and muscle until they're down to the bare bone.'

Events proved him right. Vector's breakeven was driven down, its profitability improved, there was a generous dividend, the P/E benefited. The second tranche of redundancies, however, reinforced the impression that TCP was out for every penny it could get.

To the outside world, the takeover of Vector by TCP was a success story, the type of success story that comes second only in the public eye to dramatic collapse. No public eye, however, was present to see that if things had been bad in Vector under the old management, in many ways they had scarcely improved.

'Sure, the other lot were a bunch of carpetbaggers, fleecing this company for all it was worth,' Simon Smedley, a production supervisor, confided to his fiancée. 'but TCP try to run it as though it's a bloody machine.' He laughed bitterly. 'Not that they know the half of it.' 'What's to be done?' Sandra asked. Simon shrugged. 'Not a lot,' he retorted. 'We're traumatized.'

DISCUSSION

As Simon has noted, people at Vector are traumatized. Years of lacklustre management have demotivated them. The aggressive takeover by TCP has turned their world upside down. Certainly they have seen change; equally certainly, they are dissatisfied with it. The mergers and acquisitions boom in the 1980s saw many takeover operations of this type. What has happened at Vector is more typical than rare.

What has happened at Vector? Simply put, TCP has regarded Vector as a piece of plant or machinery – an asset which must be sweated. But Vector is more than an asset or even a collection of physical assets; it is also an organization of people.

When one company takes over another, it is rare for there not to be almost tribal experiences of victory and defeat. Almost always, members of the winning company feel aggressive and victorious. Conversely, members of the losing company tend to feel beaten and subdued. Does this matter? Morally it should matter, and, from a business point of view, a demoralized workforce is hardly the most worthwhile asset.

What could TCP have done? It could have treated people at Vector as equals. It could have begun a series of regular communication meetings with the people of Vector. It could probably have provided much more reassurance than it did.

Is this realistic, one might ask? If the management at Vector was of poor quality then a tough issue needed to be addressed. But was it really necessary to replace rather than redevelop so many managers? Might the new brooms have been overzealous in their sweeping?

Another tough issue was overstaffing. Again it might have been possible to redevelop people rather than simply get rid of them. (Could new markets and business opportunities be explored?) Even if the worst is truly unavoidable, the way in which it is handled is of paramount importance. People are not fools. If a business is overstaffed, they will be fully aware of it. A clearly unavoidable rationalization process where people are treated with dignity and helped to find other work will be deemed unpalatable but fair. Throwing people on the scrap heap will ensure bitterness on the part of the victims and invoke acute self-preservation on the part of the survivors.

The latter is exactly what has happened at Vector. Financial results have improved but, with a highly motivated workforce, they might improve much more.

ater weight needs to be given to the integration of people within Vector/TCP. The
lation of Vector should be treated as a planned change process in its own right.
hologist could be seconded to Vector to help people cope with experiences of
, loss, anguish and trauma. Secondment of Vector people to TCP and vice versa
would help mutual understanding. Communication, empathy and humanity are
essentials. As is often the case where people are concerned, what is morally right also
makes sound business sense.

KEY POINTS

○   A takeover is a particular type of change process. Most takeovers are poorly
       managed.
○   Whatever the degree of integration, people at both companies need to be
       informed of it as soon as possible.
○   Magnanimity needs to be displayed. Creating 'winners and losers' is bad for
       business.
○   If harsh changes are unavoidable, they should be made as quickly and
       humanely as possible – not in tranches.
○   Outside professional help should be sought.

PRINCIPLE

Successful change requires superlative people skills.

'Get your tanks off my lawn...'

❖

Adele Fisher, the Chairwoman of Gaia, swivelled in her seat and transfixed Joe New with her beady gaze. Joe groaned inwardly. Another awkward question.

'Joe, we love your approach ...' She's softening me up, Joe decided. 'But I've got a few caveats I'd like to put to you.' Oh no, he thought. Here it comes.

'Despite our name and despite our highly environmentalist image, we have, in many ways, a very traditional company.' Adele shrugged. 'Cards on the table ... the name change was my doing – and it had to be forced through. Many would argue that our environmentalism arrived with me also.

'My instinct, our bottom line and your conclusions all say the same thing. We've got to change. I fully agree with you – we haven't got a proper infrastructure for innovation. And I like your team development approach to problem diagnosis and design.'

She hesitated. 'I'm not trying to tell you your business. But I think you may find that resistance to change is more consid-erable than currently appears.'

'Resistance to change?' Joe practically beamed. 'But that's our forte.'

Four months passed. Diagnosis was over. Design was over. The honeymoon was quite definitely over. True to what Joe called his methodology, teams had been formed at each level of the organization and across different levels. Each team had well-defined roles, tasks and terms of reference; the teams fitted together into a corporate rationale. Everything looked wonderful – on paper.

Back in the real world, everything was far from wonderful. Trying to integrate the teams was disastrously akin to bringing warring tribes together. Intra-team conflict was as pronounced as inter-team conflict. The directors sniped at each other. Middle managers felt trapped between those above and those below. With a substantial devolution of autonomy to the shop floor, supervisors felt similarly trapped. It was, in the considered opinion of Fred Lawson, the shop steward, 'a right bugger's muddle and make no mistake'.

Things finally came to a head when the

D factory action team reported to Syd Barrett, the production manager. He sat through their presentation with mounting resentment. As diagnosis followed idea and proposal followed diagnosis, he grew progressively angrier. Finally he exploded.

'I suppose you think you're being very clever about all this – you and those bloody consultants ! You've taken over my area without so much as a by your leave. Well, if you think you can run it better than I can then good luck to you. But right now I'm in post. And what I'm saying to you is this – get your tanks off my lawn!'

In vain, members of the action team protested that there had never been any attempt to usurp Syd's authority. 'And we did consult with you at the beginning,' he was reminded. This was akin to dowsing Syd's fire with petrol.

DISCUSSION

Resistance to change is a cliché; we talk about it too much and think about it too little. Then we become embroiled in it.

Change, by its very nature, brings uncertainty of process and outcome. What is happening and what is it leading to? How will it (selfishly) affect me? If push comes to shove, will I be all right?

Resistance to change should always be considered in detail at the beginning of a project. To some degree, it can be anticipated. As prevention is better than rework, it's better to elicit issues of resistance, conflict and politics at the beginning and work on them. The fact is that they will have to be worked at during every stage of a project and especially in the implementation phase.

The notion that individuals and teams will somehow get on with developing improvements for the greater good of the company is a strikingly naive one. They won't.

People need education about resistance, conflict and politics – long before tanks end up on lawns. They need to know that resistance, conflict and politics are thoroughly normal and, indeed, inevitable. They need concepts to work with, to understand such notions at a better level than cliché. And they need forums where such notions can legitimately be discussed.

Great care needs to be taken to ensure that there are not winners and losers. Everyone needs to be a winner. Conflict at all levels must be resolved, especially conflict at senior levels. Improvements generated by project teams need to be well integrated into the management structure. Such improvements need to derive from internal client needs and wants – not be imposed. There is a constant need for tact, delicacy, sensitivity and vigilance.

Change is the pathway from the past to the future. As Bob Marley sang, it must be 'in that great future we can forget the past'. Creating such a future requires rare and precious skills.

he sings
we can't forget the
past! !!

KEY POINTS

○ Resistance to change is normal and inevitable. People need to understand this.
○ Prevention is better than cure. Resistance to change thrives in darkness. Openness and education can help to dissolve it.
○ People need appropriately skilled help in resolving the myriad issues thrown up by change.

PRINCIPLE

Much of the challenge of successfully managing change lies in helping people overcome their resistance to it.

'It's industrial anarchy...'

❖

'Quite clearly, we need to change our management style,' Matthew Greenwood summarized. 'This place has had years and years of autocratic management. Let's face it – it was run practically as a military institution.'

'Well, it was successful, Matt, let's not forget that,' Roger Feely interpolated. 'But that's my whole point,' Matthew shot back. 'It was successful in spite of itself, not because of itself.

'What did we have? Layer upon layer of managers; a chain of command for the simplest decision. A managing director who used to come down on the shop floor and fix machines himself. And a cosy commercial situation of near monopoly and cost-plus pricing which meant that just about any management style would work.

'And what have we got today? No monopoly, no cost-plus, a radically delayered management structure and the worst recession of this century. We can't afford a passive workforce to come in, slave away on the tools and generally act as the

morons that we've conditioned them to be. The future's a simple either/or. Either we make drastic improvements to become competitive in a horrendous market or we all go out of business. As simple as that.'

The following months saw feverish activity as Matthew struggled to explain why routine decision-making had to be devolved to the shop floor, why improvements were no longer desirable but mandatory and why they had to fight their way through the recession together. As might be expected, after forty years of autocratic management, Matthew's message sounded strange to many.

'It's almost like prison reform,' he said wearily one evening. 'Our chaps are like prisoners who have been told to do this and do that for years. Now we're asking them for constructive input and they're not interested. They want to remain prisoners; we can't afford that.'

Shortly afterwards, he asked a management development expert to run a few sessions on communication. Great emphasis was placed on the virtues of openness and trust. 'If we're not open with each other,' she pointed out, 'we're holding back what's most important. And that will block progress.'

Emboldened by this message, Matthew retained her services and made sure that everyone on site, without exception, went through two days of training.

Six months later, the plant was in a state of disarray. The former autocracy had been replaced by a consensus management which meant that the slightest initiative had to be seemingly endlessly debated. Matthew was livid. 'It's crazy,' he said to Roger. 'What we've got is industrial anarchy. The improvements aren't coming through fast enough to save us. I'm in a cleft stick. Either we carry on with an increasingly permissive style of management – or lack of it – and somehow make things work or we revert to autocracy – which can't work. Heads we won't win; tails we lose.'

DISCUSSION

Openness and trust are indeed important, but the simple fact is that we rarely totally trust another person and we are equally rarely completely open with them. All of us have parts of ourselves which we do not wish to share with others. We all fear vulnerability because we all fear hurt. In most organizations, there is considerable interpersonal blockage which results in communication breakdown and lack of progress. Change initiatives must address such issues if they are to be successful.

Instead of attempting total openness – which will never happen anyway – it's best to opt for 'tactical openness', a limited increase in openness which is in everyone's interests. When people derive benefits and avoid penalties through being encourged to be tactically open about mutual problems, they will be prepared to be more readily open the next time around. Success, however small, needs to be built upon success and communicated. Nothing succeeds quite like a record of success.

Quite obviously, Matthew and his fellow directors have opted for openness in communication and management style without sufficiently thinking it through. Tactical openness is the way forward in communication. Controlled devolution of power is the way forward in terms of management style. New roles must be carefully negotiated so that autocracy is not replaced by anarchy. Interestingly, Matthew was strikingly autocratic about the training sessions. Has he reflected upon this?

The training sessions are utterly inadequate and are pitched at a symptom level rather than a causal level. There are much deeper problems which need to be worked through before operational improvements are here to stay.

KEY POINTS

O   Most, if not all, organizations are composed of people who are interpersonally blocked through unresolved conflict.

O   Such interpersonal blockage generates lack of openness and trust. These, in turn, inhibit change.

O   Encouraging limited tactical increases in openness and trust is a better way forward than saintly pretences of complete openness. Mutual success is the best encouragement.

O   Roles and changes in roles need to be carefully negotiated. Controlled change, not anarchy, is needed.

O   Where significant interpersonal blockage remains, it must be resolved.

PRINCIPLE

Tactical openness is almost always necessary for successful change.

'We told them all right – we just didn't communicate...'

❖

Above the doorway of the boardroom of Plexus Engineering, the clock stood at five minutes to one. Unanimously the board approved 'the introduction of new working practices designed to foster a more proactive culture'. Relieved, they trooped out in search of lunch. The clock stood at one....

Industry specialists had emphasized the importance of keeping the employees of Plexus fully informed as to what such new working practices might entail. Open communication was anathema to many in Plexus, who tended to operate on the old military adage of 'tell 'em only what (we think) they need to know'.

However, in an effort to be fair to all concerned, the board, after due union consultation, issued a letter to each employee, appraising them of the proposed changes. This was backed up by sessions with 'the troops' in the works canteen. Again an old military maxim was employed: 'Tell 'em what you're going to say. Say it. Then tell 'em what you've said.' Naturally there was an opportunity for questions from the floor. Several audiences proved embarrassingly silent. A few people asked rather obvious questions. One doughty individual, upon questioning whether the proposed changes really were the best way forward for the company, was tersely advised to 'Do your job and leave our's to us.'

On the agreed dates, the changes in working practices were duly implemented. While everybody expected some disruption, few were prepared for the wholesale upheaval which resulted. One old-timer, of unquestionable loyalty, bitterly reflected, 'These changes in working practices have set us back ten years.'

Management was affronted. 'It just goes to show,' remarked one board member. 'You try to do your best for people. You put them in the picture. You tell them what's going on. And do they support you? Do they hell! We might as well have not bothered telling them in the first place.'

'It's a bad business,' a fellow board member agreed. 'I well remember the day we made the initial decision. I had my doubts then but of course I didn't want to appear negative.'

DISCUSSION

The best definition of communication is 'mutual understanding'. Telling people something is no guarantee of communication. For a start, it is one way. Furthermore, it ignores checking to see whether they've understood. And even if they have understood, do you know what they're thinking? Not unless they tell you.

Communication – as mutual understanding – inevitably requires discussion. Discussion of such an important initiative as changes in working practices will always take place. One cannot stop people thinking (internal discussion) or talking. By giving employees ample opportunity for public discussion in structured sessions, many of the more pernicious effects of the grapevine can be avoided.

The silent audiences, however, testify to the lack of history of productive dialogue between management and workforce at Plexus. Mutually productive discussion of such an important issue as changes in working practices requires established avenues of communication – which clearly do not yet exist.

The directors of Plexus are not convinced of the importance of communication. Therefore they have merely been going through the motions. And it shows. My, how it shows. They are actually communicating a very powerful message indeed, one which says, 'We're pretending to have an open communication session. In reality, we're telling you. We're not really interested in your views.' Such non-verbal messages are very well understood. They invite silences which contain counter-messages, such as, 'We think that this communication session is a confidence trick,' or even, 'We don't care about our company.'

We live in an era of ever more open communication. Generally, people want free and frank discussion. The industrial passivity of earlier generations has largely vanished. While 'need to know' may be applicable in the military, in civilian organizations 'want to know' is usually more apt. The sessions with 'the troops' were an early indication that all was not as it should be. The board of Plexus would have done well to heed such an ill omen.

The board should have started with itself. Has it communicated (mutually understood) the nature of the proposed changes? Not on the evidence of at least one member who had (justified?) doubts and yet held back. Perhaps the poor chap who spoke out had some relevant points to make. Maybe he was simply trying to be pertinent – not impertinent, after all.

KEY POINTS

○ Communication as mutual understanding means much more than merely telling people.

○ Change requires commitment, not just passive agreement. This means considerable discussion.

○   Such discussion tends to be time-consuming. Busy managers have the choice: take the time now or lose it later.

○   If there are no mechanisms for discussion, they will have to be created – again time-consuming, again necessary.

PRINCIPLE

Successful change requires superlative communication.

'There aren't any measurable improvements...'

❖

'We Don't Have Customers – We Have Clients' – the desk-top published document from central marketing services obviously viewed the parks department in a somewhat different light than did Joe Witherspoon, the Murgatroyd supervisor. Crouched over an oil fire in the cabin he shared with his five lads, he spat derisively and with considerable accuracy. 'Clients! Don't make me laugh!' he scoffed, before flinging the offending publication into the bin. His 'lads' – the eldest of whom was over forty – looked on with scant interest. Presently a pack of cards was produced.

Events assumed a more sinister turn, however, when Joe's presence was requested on what turned out to be a series of weekend sessions with 'the top brass and their flunkeys'. Joe's first reaction was swift and to the point. 'What's in it for me?' he demanded of his union rep. On hearing that he would be paid overtime and that the food was good, he reluctantly agreed to go.

'Games!' he sneered, the following Monday. 'Grown men playing bloody games. "Design Your New Organization",' he brutally mimicked. '"Seven Exercises To Tell Whether Your Culture's Right".' 'Culture, Joe?' one of the lads queried. 'Aye, lad – culture!' was the dismissive reply. 'Tha' knows – brass bands and string quartets.'

The year wore on much as the previous year had done and the one before that. Joe attended more 'little events', as he grew to call them. Once the director of recreation herself came down to the park on an unofficial visit. 'Best make the most of it, lads,' Joe chided, 'We've not seen her before and we'll not see her again.'

'Obviously, we've got a long way to go,' Paul Simpkiss, of Policy Development, carefully remarked, shortly after Christmas. 'Some of these characters have been with the parks department for all of their working lives. They're not going to come round to our way of thinking, just like that.'

'So what's your policy?' interrupted Hugo Riley, a prominent local academic. 'Hearts and minds?' he caustically suggested. Simpkiss affected dispassion.

'Hearts and minds ... I suppose you might call it that,' he carefully acknowledged. He frowned. 'We regard it as an educational process – a continuing dialogue between ourselves, our staff and our clients.' 'Clients?' Riley queried, much as Witherspoon had before him. 'Clients,' Simpkiss firmly replied, although he flushed vividly.

'And your clients? Have they obtained improvements since this process began?' 'Yes, I rather fancy they have.'

'Measurable improvements?' Riley swiftly interposed. 'No, not measurable,' Simpkiss conceded. 'Well, what about your staff? Are they starting to deliver such improvements?' 'Not yet!' Simpkiss snapped. 'We think it's a little early.'

Meanwhile, back in the cabin, Witherspoon chortled at the latest handout. A weekend at Charlton Grange. The grub there was reputed to be excellent. He could really get to like this change lark.

DISCUSSION

To date, there have not been any measurable improvements. Nor, if Joe has his way, will there ever be.

There have been no measurable improvements because the parks department has neglected the importance of measurable improvements. Rather, it has construed its change programme as being primarily educational.

In adopting such a stance, it has succeeded in ensuring that the necessary expenditure will be viewed as cost, not investment. When the finance committee impose the next round of spending cuts, it is highly likely that this change process will be one of the casualties. Its premature demise will destroy even the possibility of change in the parks department. It may be many years before progress is again attempted.

Why has the parks department not focused upon measurable improvements? There are several likely answers. One is sheer naivety on the part of those who should know better. There is probably also a fear that to specify measurable improvements will lay people open to charges of incompetence should these improvements not appear. Finally there may be genuine ignorance in defining operational measures which can be improved.

Highlighting worthwhile results is apt to be a fraught affair. The management by objectives movement in the 1960s focused upon the achievement of measurable improvements. Unfortunately the movement was discredited by massaged measures being achieved in a massaged manner. Most companies' appraisal schemes are similarly flawed to this day.

People need to consider what the parks department actually does, why it does it and what (if anything) it seeks to achieve. This would generate the parks department's mission in general terms and its goals in specific measures. The goals would themselves break down into contributory operational targets. It could then be considered how these targets might be improved and to what extent.

Ironically, such language, while probably not over-welcome, would be readily understood by Joe and his lads. There would still be a need for an educational process to broaden people's horizons. In fact, it would be highly desirable if the parks department staff themselves worked out their mission, goals and targets. The end result would be both tangible and relevant. And one can focus upon tangibles in a way that one cannot focus on generalities.

Along the way, Joe's cynicism and self-interest would have to be tackled. How many Joes are there? Why are they so cynical? Is it all their own doing or might the parks department foster cynicism? How much do they and it need to change?

The cosmetic shift to 'clients' is all very well, but raise these clients' expectations and there will be vociferous cries for improved delivery. The parks department had better make sure that it can and does deliver.

KEY POINTS

○   A well-designed change process will necessarily be educational and developmental.

○   If, however, such a process does not also focus upon operational improvement then why go through it?

○   If such improvement is not measurable, then how can anyone know if and when it has occurred?

○   Mission, goals and targets are best decided by the people within an organization (with outside facilitation). They, after all, are the people who will have to deliver the results.

PRINCIPLE

Change without results is no change at all.

'Things are getting worse, not better...'

❖

Positron Equipment made electronic components for industrial users. The main manufacturing plant had grown like Topsy in the boom years. Now, with the spectre of recession hanging over the country, parts of the rabbit warren were conspicuously silent.

'We thought the downturn would at least help us rationalize our manufacturing process,' Gwen Masters, the works manager, explained to Alice Young of Youngblood Consulting, 'But I'm afraid that doesn't seem to have been the case. It's just as hard getting orders through the plant as it's ever been.' She hesitated. 'We've got a good product; everybody acknowledges that. But our lead times have historically been poor. We've always had difficulty meeting due dates. Now,' she shrugged ruefully, 'we can't afford late deliveries. Not with possible over-supply in the market. If we can't produce the goods in time, someone else will.'

The Youngblood analysis of Positron began that week. It rapidly became apparent that production planning was ad hoc and ill informed. Production control was noticeable by its absence. If fact, as one of the Youngblood consultants pointed out to Alice, when she came on site to find out how the analysis was progressing, 'The only way to get product across this factory floor and out the door is to expedite it.'

'The trouble is, of course,' he continued, 'that's exactly what everyone does. Machine centres start processing an order which they know full well will be interrupted time and again as other, more favoured orders are slipped in ahead of it. Extra machine set-up times, multiple handling, inventory, work in progress and finished stock all over the place. It's a regular cat's cradle.'

'Systems,' Alice told Gwen at the analysis presentation. 'This place needs systems. Forecasting, planning and control systems. Systems to bring order into chaos.'

'Yes, I daresay you're right,' Gwen agreed, 'but we've had systems before and I'm bound to say, they haven't worked.' 'Believe me,' Alice assured her, 'this time they will.'

Shortly afterwards, the project began.

The first phase of systems design involved the consultants asking a great many more questions from a wide variety of personnel. On the shop floor, life continued as before; product was still being expedited. When the project moved into its next phase, however, disruption was plain for all to see. Productivity nosedived, lead times got even longer, key shipments were missed. Finally Gwen telephoned Alice. 'I'll come straight to the point, Alice,' she said. 'We started off this exercise in good faith. But things are getting worse, not better.'

DISCUSSION

It is an old truism that things get worse before they get better; unfortunately, in change projects, this is almost always the case.

Positron has a cultural value which says, 'expedite product'. People have been doing it for years and it has become an accepted way of life. It will certainly take more than a few weeks for people to stop one way of working and adopt another.

The choice at Positron is plain. People can continue their historical approach of ad hoc planning and management. If they do this, they run a high chance of losing market share, with dramatic consequences in a downturn. This is not a viable option. Alternatively, people can begin to work in a more systematic and professional manner. This requires discipline – and the best discipline is self-discipline.

Quite evidently, people at Positron have lacked self-discipline in the past. By Gwen's own admission, there have been previous systems installations which have failed. Unless something radically different happens this time, the present approach will also fail.

By adopting systems, Positron is curtailing flexibility (which in truth is near-anarchy) for the greater good. In effect, this means that an overall production plan is too important to be sacrificed for any order, no matter how urgent it might be. Imposing a production plan and slipping in specials is a recipe for disaster. Yet this is exactly what is happening – resulting in the worst of all possible worlds. Of course salespeople will come into the factory to try to get their special orders slipped through. Of course the sales director will argue at the weekly production meeting that the system is too rigid and should be altered to cater to the demands of a key customer – a different one, each week.

Two elements are lacking. There is a lack of appreciation of how this cultural value of expediting has arisen historically – and what its consequences are. There is also a lack of an educational process whereby people can understand that continually expediting product has an adverse impact on job satisfaction, resource usage and working capital. In short, it is a way of working which Positron can no longer afford.

People also need to understand that, no matter what the case for a new *modus operandi*, behavioural change is going to be the hard part. Unlearning old habits while learning new ones is likely to result in even worse performance in the short term. People must be consulted, allowances must be made – between production staff, with other departments, especially with customers. If discipline is maintained, the short-term dip in performance will be vindicated by diminished lead times, better productivity and increased job satisfaction. Then, and not before, will the hard work be worth it.

KEY POINTS

○ Change needs an educational platform. People must understand why change is necessary, both in broad terms and in specific terms.

○ Change must ultimately become behavioural. People must begin to behave differently.

○ Behaving differently means unlearning old habits while learning new ones. Performance will intially drop; with success, it will dramatically improve.

PRINCIPLE

Performance drops with change; with successful change, it dramatically improves.

'We declared UDI...'

❖

Pete Crew arrived at Alpha Financial Services with one aim in mind – improved performance in as short a space of time as humanly possible. 'That's my job and, by jiminy, I'm going to do it,' he said. His previous career had been in marketing – he had launched the biggest unit trust ever, unfortunately coinciding with the 1987 stock market crash. 'There's timing for you,' he had toasted himself without remorse; then moved on.

Pete had always worked in marketing and saw his general managership as the vital rung on a promotional ladder which would propel him into the ranks of senior management within the financial services industry. His approach to working life was simple: 'Work hard and play hard.' Stock market crashes excepted, it had served him well.

Pete had been brought into the corporate products division on a change ticket. 'The place needs change; you seem the sort of chap to get it,' he'd been informed at interview. Pete's first act was formally to address all of his staff. 'I'm a simple sort of chap,' he mildly told them. 'I work hard and play hard. If we all do the same, then we can really make this place zing!'

And 'zing' it did, in the months to come. People responded to Pete's infectious enthusiasm. An element came back into their work which had been absent for longer than they could remember – fun.

However, 'Pete's antics' were regarded as anything but funny at head office, inconveniently situated just across the road. 'He's setting precedents over there, dangerous precedents.' Pete, for his part, refused to lunch in any of the seven hierarchically arranged management dining rooms. 'I haven't got time for any of that nonsense,' he maintained.

'A friendly word in your ear, Pete,' Roy Harper, his deputy, suggested one evening, after their twice-weekly workout at the local gym. 'Tone it down, for heaven's sake. This latest move towards profit-related pay is really shaking them up across the road.' 'Huh! That's because we're making profits and they're not,' Pete scoffed. 'Maybe so,' Roy concurred, 'but they're saying that we're declaring UDI.' 'Maybe we should at that,' replied Pete.

Pete was not aware that Roy had been promised the general managership before him. Roy dutifully, and with immense concealed glee, reported back to his political masters across the road. They were unanimous in their verdict. 'The chap's got one last chance and then that's it. UDI indeed!'

Pete's last chance came and went. When he was given twenty minutes to clear his desk, it surprised no one except him. A pity, everyone said. Such a pleasant fellow.

DISCUSSION

Pete, to his credit, knew what he came to do and had the integrity to get on with it. He had come from the 'work hard, play hard' atmosphere of successful, self-contained marketing departments and had yet to realize that being a general manager means coming into contact with a much wider range of motivations and temperaments. In time, he might have learned.

Pete's approach to change was equally unsophisticated, but his friendliness, accessibility and devotion won him many allies. Bringing fun back into people's working lives is no mean achievement.

Pete's highly task-oriented nature, which was his strength, was also his weakness. A wiser person would, from the outset, have queried whether he was being set up. Was Pete being set up? He will never know, but it's a distinct possibility. Many organizations send out mixed messages. 'Yes, we want change but we also want the status quo. We want innovation but we also want a safe pair of hands.'

Pete certainly dramatically mismanaged the political nature of his role. He mismanaged it because he despised organizational politics. Whatever one feels about such politics, the plain fact is that they always exist. The more senior the position, the more likely it is that one will have to spend a significant amount of one's time dealing with politics.

If change has not happened in the past, it's always wise to question why it hasn't happened, i.e. what forces may be ranged against it? Had Pete more nous, he might have uncovered a wide array of forces ranged against the very kind of change that he was brought in to implement. Along the way, he might have developed his suspicions about other people, perhaps even his close cohort and training buddy, Roy.

Instead of being labelled with UDI, Pete should have negotiated a role for corporate products *vis-à-vis* head office – a role which would have balanced the conflicting needs for autonomy and control. Within this role, he could have mobilized a team who would inspire change within corporate products. As well as escaping the UDI tag, he would have also have avoided the one-man-band tag.

To negotiate such a role would have meant continued dialogue with his senior managers at head office. Whatever Pete felt about them, they were the people in post and the people with whom he needed to deal. To remove the dining rooms would require power; ironically, Pete needed to eat in them in the first place to acquire such power.

As it is, Pete's progress to senior management has received a severe setback and a potentially sound piece of development work has been terminated. (Watch what happens to fun when Roy takes over.)

KEY POINTS

○   Organizational politics is a reality in every organization, at every time. Ignore it at your peril.

○   The more senior your position, the more your need to learn to manage politics.

○   The process of change is irretrievably political; it must therefore be politically managed.

PRINCIPLE

Management is political; change is much more so.

'Somebody mugged our baby...'

❖

'What I'd like you to do,' Sylvia McElroy said, 'is list all the factors which could put you out of business.' 'That's easy,' replied Ben Moon, the site general manager. 'Pollution.' 'Pollution?' Sylvia queried. 'Pollution,' Ben replied. 'If we don't get our act together, we'll be out of business in five years.'

'All right then,' Sylvia replied, writing on the communal flip chart. 'So what else is there?' she prompted. Ben frowned. 'Pollution. No, honestly, Sylvia, that really is our prime concern.'

Externally calm, Sylvia inwardly sighed. Oh yes, just about anyone can be a process consultant, she mordantly reflected.

'"A way of seeing is a way of not seeing",' she quoted. 'Oh, Sylvia, you're getting all philosophical on us again,' Graeme smilingly protested. Sylvia grinned. 'Maybe I am. But as long as we're thinking about pollution, we're probably missing a host of other factors which could equally put us out of business. For instance –' She listed three, any one of which might have finished the plant overnight. 'And, guys,

you know your business. I don't. There have got to be other factors. And we'd better identify them.' Ben and Graeme looked at each other, light dawning, all levity suddenly gone. 'I ... see what you mean,' Ben slowly admitted. It was half acknowledgement, half apology.

They ended up with 'Six factors that could kill us' on the flip chart. Prematurely satisfied, they leaned back to proffer solutions. 'Hang on a moment,' Sylvia protested. Slowly, carefully, she wrote one more word on the flip chart, one more potential killer. The room became silent. 'Insiders.'

'You're a local site with a great deal of local autonomy,' she explained, 'but you're also part of a conglomerate. We're talking serious culture change here. People out there – powerful people – mightn't like it, mightn't understand it, might feel directly or indirectly threatened by it. That's something else for you to manage. If we don't get the results, they'll put a stop to this change process, probably mothball the site into the bargain. But when we do get the results,

95

there will be a lot of so-called sceptics out there who will suddenly want to be associated with them. You don't need an airline ticket to get hijacked,' she drily observed.

Ben never forgot that workshop. 'It changed my life,' he said, long afterwards. 'It really did.' The three-year change programme restored the plant to prof- itability, saved hundreds of jobs in a depressed region, and transformed dozens of lives.

It was nearly five years before Sylvia's grim warning came true. In a boardroom in Milan, she was passed a note with Ben's terse message. 'We should have listened harder. You were right. Somebody mugged our baby.'

DISCUSSION

Organizations are political places. Like it or not, enemies and predators are not all outside; invariably some of them are within. A few will not intend to be enemies or predators; usually, however, they will have sharply divergent views which need to be integrated and which often can yield considerable value. Some will be jungle creatures which need to be captured and tamed. Others need to be exterminated. Organizations are political places....

Managers are paid to manage. Senior managers are paid to manage not a particular function but whatever comes along. The existence of politics means that they need to manage politics also.

Nowhere is this more important than in change processes which, by their very nature, involve political shifts. Backing is always needed from the board of directors, from above the board and from below the board. Typically, change processes involve a laying down of arms between warring factions. This requires neutral zones whose neutrality must be rigorously protected through ceaseless vigilance.

Ben heeded Sylvia's warning, but he didn't heed it well enough. For three years, she kept him vigilant, but even she couldn't keep him vigilant for ever. He relaxed his guard. And, as Sylvia subsequently discovered, a wheeler-dealer from the parent company, in the process of being booted sideways, has become chairman. Paradoxically, while claiming all the credit for the results, he will attempt to implement countermeasures to negate the shift in management philosophy and thus, ironically, imperil those very results. By the time the results collapse, he will be on his way again, nimbly hopping from ice floe to ice floe, each one sinking behind him.

Ben and his companions have a fight on their hands. Their baby has been mugged. Unless appropriate protective action is implemented, a far worse fate awaits it.

KEY POINTS

○   Organizations are political places. Predators and enemies can lurk on the inside as well as the outside.

○   Senior managers are paid to manage politics, enemies from within or without, and whatever else may emerge.

○   Change processes involve highly sophisticated political skills – not for engaging in spurious politics but for creating appropriate conditions for peace and progress.

○   Change is a delicate flower which often needs protection to bloom.

○   It's better to be unceasingly vigilant than to suffer a hijack.

PRINCIPLE

Management is political; change is much, much more so.

'We've restructured...'

❖

'Gentlemen, the good days are gone. Insurance claims have rocketed in the last three years. Premiums have gone up; volume has gone down. Public faith in financial institutions is at an all-time low. The public used to view us as bastions of probity. Now at best they regard us as supermarkets of financial services, at worst, well....'

David Jenkins, the new broom, looked around him at the other members of his top team. Fear. The room reeked of fear. Well, so be it.

'The competition's increasing. Our costs are too high. We need to restructure.' At mention of the dreaded 'R' word, a collective sigh of acquiescence was exhaled. Well, at least now they knew. The axe would fall; probably it would fall on some of them. In the depths of recession, there was no hope of golden handshakes. But, perhaps, bronze handshakes?

The months to come were traumatic. A big-name management consultancy went through the organization 'like a dose of salts', as one middle manager ruefully put it. Too many layers of management, too many staff canteens, too much duplication of internal services. Yesterday's seeming necessities were today's unaffordable luxuries.

Costs went down; losses dwindled. Slowly, the long climb to breakeven began. But operations didn't improve; if anything, they got worse.

'Never seen it so bad,' Bill Marley confided to Ron Baslow, one evening after work as they stopped for a quick pint in the pub opposite the railway station. 'Morale's rock bottom as you might expect. But it's not just that. We've restructured but now nobody knows what they should be doing. The old chain of command was so long that people just saw a tiny piece of the action. Now people have to take a broader view. But I don't think they can. Either they focus on a tiny piece, as before, and let all the other pieces run rampage, or they try to juggle all of them.' He sighed heavily. 'It's the devil and the deep blue sea. I'm not saying that we didn't have to restructure, I'm not saying that at all. But,' he groped for words, the right words, 'but we haven't changed fundamentally – and that's what we need to do. All right, David Jenkins has got himself a result and we're edging back into profit – so that can't be bad. But our operations are a right mess and I'm damned if I know what to do about it.'

Ron looked at the minute hand of the clock above the Edwardian saloon bar. 'Fancy another, then?' 'Oh aye,' Bill agreed. 'Why not? I don't mind if I do.'

DISCUSSION

There are few organizations which have not been 'restructured' in the 1980s and early 1990s; many of them will have been through the experience repeatedly.

Restructuring tends to be a euphemism for cost-cutting via people reduction. Many organizations are under severe pressure to reduce variable costs. A classic cost to pounce on is people costs. An analogy can be drawn with dieting. Many organizations, like many people, are or were overweight. Going on a diet loses weight; not changing one's eating habits ensures that the weight comes straight back on again afterwards. So is it with cost reduction. Fat goes; often muscle goes also. Health and fitness may suffer. But have eating habits changed?

People who know little about organizational change and development compulsively talk about organizational structure. They imply that if you get the structure right then everything else will somehow come right too. This is rarely so.

Changing the structure will not automatically change the process, i.e. what people actually do. Simply promoting the top salesperson to sales manager will not necessarily make that person behave any differently. They now occupy a different place in the structure, but a different process? Change? Far more likely that they will carry on behaving in super-salesperson mode.

The middle manager who has been promoted to department head and company director may confuse the two roles and retain a parochialism which negates both. A different place in the structure, yes; change, no.

Similarly, a whole organization can be restructured and the only change may be numerical (fewer people) and negative (less being done). Those who have been restructured may not have changed their processes. Their job titles are different but they don't understand their roles (their functional relationships with others) and their skills refer to the past. This is a recipe for operational disaster. Unfortunately, it is a common situation among organizations of all types, who confuse quantitative change with qualitative change. Unless people are encouraged to develop, they will become incompetent in their new functions.

In companies such as our finance organization, where people's spheres of responsibility are much wider, there is even more need for development. The roles must be clarified – preferably by the people occupying them. Accountabilities must be set, people must be able to evaluate their performance, and they should be given help to do all of these things.

Changing the structure may or may not be part of a change process. By itself, it will achieve little of value.

KEY POINTS

○ Structure is where people are in the organization; process is what they do and how they do it. The two should never be confused.

○ The key to both structure and process is role. Role defines people in terms of their functional relationships. This is a pragmatic approach rather than a theoretical one.

○ Change always involves process (behaviour). It may, or may not, involve structure.

○ Process change is developmental. People need suitable professional help.

PRINCIPLE

True change is about reprocessing (new behaviour), rather than merely restructuring (different jobs).

'You don't know shit from Shinola!'

❖

'A smokestack industry... I suppose we are, really,' Simon Beaumont reflected. 'And one of the few of this size still left in private hands. But we'd better put our house in order while we've still got a house at all.'

Hedera was a heavy engineering company based in Doncaster. Family-owned, it had prospered, declined, staged an all too brief recovery and declined once more. The imperatives were simple – reduce costs, improve quality, shorten lead times. Achieving them was hard.

Acting on an impulse (some might say whim), Simon invited over Laura Harding, the CEO of their American operation. Laura was one of the few of her Harvard MBA year who had gone into manufacturing as her daddy and grandaddy had before her. Hell, she loved production!

She did not love what she found at Hedera. Antiquated systems, 'behind the times' working practices, busy, busy people. Laura's lip curled and she fought not to say it. 'Firefighting.'

'Start with the people, not the process,' she said. They did. 'Get someone good in to help you,' she said. They did.

Six months later, a company-wide change programme was under way. A task force reported to the main board and devolved into action teams. The task force highlighted improvements; the action teams implemented them. Progress was being made; people were beginning to sound enthusiastic.

So it came as quite a surprise when Laura next visited the site. 'Fine. What you guys are doing is fine. You're getting improvements. But what you're not doing is managing the core business. And you need to do that as well – in fact, more so.'

'I'm sorry Laura,' Simon admitted. 'I'm afraid you've rather lost me.' There was a murmur of assent round the boardroom table. Laura sighed, breathed deeply. 'Hell, it's my fault. Should have seen it before. You haven't got the information to manage the business. You've got three accountancy-based computer systems which don't talk to each other. They're as irrelevant as they're incompatible. You need management control information – the right information, for the right people at the right time. That way, they can make the right decisions – and thereby develop.'

'Laura, you seem to be suggesting that we're not in control, that we don't know what's going on,' Frank Willoughby, the production director, testily responded. Laura looked at him coolly, levelly. 'Frank,' she said softly, 'the information simply isn't there. Therefore the control can't be there either. So don't try to con me. You don't know shit from Shinola!'

DISCUSSION

It looks as though World War III is ready to begin! But, seriously, Laura's point is entirely valid. Many companies who want improvements think that such improvements can somehow be grafted on to normal day-to-day operations. To some extent, they can. But, if the operations aren't being effectively managed in the first place, then the improvements aren't or shouldn't be the first priority. They may even be irrelevant, a red herring distracting attention from the main issue. And, if operations aren't being managed properly, then the benefits of any improvements tend to be diluted, if not indeed lost.

All operations require control. Control is only possible with information – the right information. Management information should show output against input (and thus performance) for every person, machine centre, work area, department. For people to improve, they need to be able to measure their performance. As Laura says, for the right decisions to be made, you need the right information at the right time.

The IT infrastructure is poor, so business information is lacking. That is a problem; but it's a different problem. A management control system can be designed and installed in a fraction of the time needed for revision and upgrading of the manufacturing systems.

Management information systems (MIS) are about the process. Management control systems (MCS) are about outputs and inputs. Get MIS right and life is certainly easier. Get MCS right and you have a vehicle to develop people to get better day-to-day operations and much-needed improvements.

KEY POINTS

○   Operational improvement requires better control of day-to-day business as well as specific ad hoc improvement.
○   To get better control of day-to-day business, management control systems (MCS) are needed.
○   MCS should not be confused with MIS.
○   MCS design and development should go hand in hand with people development.

PRINCIPLE

The right change requires the right information for the right people at the right time.

'The strategy was great, but...'

❖

'One action we will not take, ladies and gentlemen, is to go into this venture with our eyes closed. I am determined that we shall take a strategic view not only of our businesses but also of this change process to which we have committed ourselves today.' Ivan Firth, the Chairman of Commix Ceramics, raised his glass of champagne. As one, the serried rows of executives did likewise. 'A toast! A toast, ladies and gentlemen ... to our new future!' 'To our new future!' they dutifully chorused.

Attaining that future, however, was more easily said than done. In the months which followed Ivan's inaugural speech, a change committee was formed, reporting to the main board and comprising the heads of the operating businesses. This committee was charged with the task of designing and implementing a change programme which would restore Commix to profitability in the near future.

Almost from the beginning, the process seemed to run into difficulties. The main board members themselves were far from unanimous about the need for a change

committee. Some saw it as an example of good delegation, others felt that, 'as the buck stops with us, we should be the change committee'. Painstakingly, Ivan explained that the change committee was an 'enabling mechanism' to make changes happen in the core businesses. 'Our role in the centre is more strategic. We need to assess which innovations best fit with the long-term future of the businesses.' 'You mean, they're like the House of Commons and we're like the House of Lords,' suggested one board member. 'You could put it like that,' Ivan doubtfully agreed.

It was readily apparent that the House of Commons and the House of Lords rarely saw eye to eye on which aspects of the businesses should be 'first in the firing line for change'. The change committee suggested a product rationalization which was promptly vetoed by the main board. The main board then suggested a productivity drive which was strenuously resisted by the change committee. 'You're in effect telling us that we're not running our own businesses properly,' they accused the main board. 'No, we're not,' the main board vigorously retorted. 'We're just telling you that productivity improvements are perfectly possible and highly desirable in your businesses.'

'There you go again,' was the inevitable reply, while one bluff Yorkshireman bluntly retorted, 'If you think there are productivity improvements to be had in my business, then bloody well go and get them yourself!' To which the prim response was, 'That's not our job.' 'Aye, well then, leave me alone to get on with mine!'

The main board and the change committee were deadlocked – much to Ivan's chagrin. In vain, the heads of the operating businesses tried to drive change beneath them. 'Impossible when nobody's sure what's going on,' one confided. 'Let's face it – the strategy was great, but....'

DISCUSSION

The strategy was anything but great. True, the strategic intent was present, but strategic intents do not, of themselves, constitute strategies. This seems to be a law of life which has so far escaped Ivan.

Ivan's choice of a change committee as a mechanism for change was sound. What he lacked both with strategy and the change committee was any kind of follow-through. In each case, he seemed to think that if he merely set things up, they would run of their own volition.

Obviously both the main board and the change committee are unsure of their own and each other's roles. The main board should be charged with the overall strategic direction of the businesses. That direction, which will be dynamic, not static, needs to be fully understood by the change committee.

Against the strategic backdrop, the operating businesses must be viewed and the questions asked – why, where and how should change occur? Once these questions have been answered, the real effort can begin – in the operating businesses where industrial battles are won and lost.

The whole adds up to a large-scale, company-wide process of understanding. There will necessarily be conflict. What is best for one particular business may impact unfavourably upon group policy. Tensions always exist between group and operating levels, head offices and divisions. Nowhere is this more apparent than in the perennial struggle between operational autonomy and tight financial control.

The change committee has certainly got a difficult job on its hands. It needs to conduct a useful dialogue with the main board – and ensure it receives much-needed support. It needs to communicate, analyse and implement within businesses, and it needs to integrate efforts so that change succeeds at an individual business level and also at a company-wide level.

The present confusion needs sharp resolution before the change process is irretrievably doomed. Ivan himself must cut through his own intellectual fog and understand that words are no substitute for deeds.

KEY POINTS

○   Change is best viewed in terms of the overall strategic direction of a company.
○   Inevitably mechanisms for change need to be created. Often these will complement the existing management structure.
○   Integration between enabling mechanisms and the management structure at all levels must be achieved.
○   Where there are conflicts or ambiguities of role, they must resolutely be clarified.

PRINCIPLE

Change requires well-considered, integrated enabling mechanisms.

'They talk a good fight...'

❖

Ralph Dangerfield might not have been everyone's cup of tea but you certainly could not accuse him of being reactionary. He had been brought in from outside as CEO of Vella TV, one of the newest and most innovative franchisees. Considering the somewhat abrupt departure of his predecessor (locks changed on the office door, five minutes to leave the building with a phalanx of security men), one might have expected a certain amount of resentment, if not *amour propre*. And, as Ralph himself admitted, 'What the hell do I know about running a TV station?' A view with which many of his employees heartily concurred.

'We're not the Beeb, so let's not even try,' he bluntly told them. 'Culture. You guys know about culture.... Well, it's got to change. Like fast. You want to see the numbers? I'll show you the numbers!'

Vella's overheads called for dramatic change. Not one to skimp, Ralph asked around. 'Emera,' they said. 'Bunch of psychologists. Yeah, I know, I know... sure, it sounds off the wall. But they're who you want.... Go for them.'

Ralph did. 'Raise awareness,' they said. Seminars on this, seminars on that. 'Get people together,' they said. Joint sessions on this, joint sessions on that. 'The power of synergy,' they said. But synergy was synergy and Ralph's cost structure remained unchanged. 'What the hell's going on?' he said. 'They talk a good fight,' he was told.

DISCUSSION

What is lacking here in two words is project management. Emera may or may not be good; Ralph's people are certainly good. And yet it's not happening. There is no operational benefit. Different realities may, or may not, be being negotiated. In the meantime, Vella is going bust.

Change is organic, not mechanistic. But change projects need a mechanistic structure. Getting the balance right is as difficult as it is vital. With mechanistic people, the emphasis is usually quantitative; with creative people, it's usually qualitative. Emera appears to fall into the latter category.

Without project management, there is no framework for progress and improved results. Change is change ... rather than specific change, with whom, by when. Project management applies a pragmatic rigour to conceptual thought. This means zero slippage project management, rather than sloppy overruns. Ralph has to pay the bills; he needs results. He doesn't want promises of eternal tomorrows. He wants delivery. It's high time he got it.

KEY POINTS

O   Culture change is organic and developmental, not mechanistic.
O   Creativity needs to be balanced by control, otherwise there is only a forever journey to a non-existent destination.
O   Project management is *de rigueur* in change projects.
O   Proper project management means zero slippage, not perennial excuses.

PRINCIPLE

Change requires superlative project management.

'We just ran out of steam...'

❖

'High hopes..., we started this thing with high hopes. And look what's come to pass. But why? Why? I've asked myself that question a thousand times. And there's always a different answer. Maybe my answers are too complicated; maybe the truth's simpler. Maybe we just ran out of steam.

'Everything seemed different then. You can't begin to imagine the excitement we used to feel. It really did seem to course through our veins. There was a sense that the whole future was up for grabs. I used to wake up each morning dying to come to work. And now,.... now we're all living from term to term.

'We were young then. Well, late thirties ... but old enough to have done things in life and young enough to still care about doing them properly. We'd grown up with terribly traditional experiences in education, experiences which had left us dramatically unprepared for the wider world. And then we'd found ourselves back in education again, running courses in management – the ultimate pragmatism – and being lumbered with these same old timeworn dogmas. We knew it wasn't right but we didn't dare challenge the prevailing orthodoxy.

'Until Paul came in as head of department.... Like us, he'd been in the middle echelons of British industry. Started life as a consulting engineer, did some good work in developing countries, before it was the done thing. He'd been around; he knew management practice through and through.

'So when he saw this drivel we were teaching, he said, "That's exactly what it is ... drivel." And then, with a sort of apologetic half-smile, "But what do you chaps think? Perhaps you can convince me otherwise."

'Of course we couldn't. And when we admitted we couldn't, he threw it straight back at us. "Then let's rip the syllabus up, and rewrite it. Let's give our students management education which will transform their careers. And their lives."

'Naturally all hell broke loose. The academic authorities were outraged. There was talk of both accreditation and funding being withdrawn. Some of the students hated it; they just wanted to pass the exams, get their little scraps of paper and continue being mediocre – but with pieces of paper. But the better students loved it. Like us, it was what they'd been longing for – management education which was about real life, not make-believe.

'We fought our battles and we won them – because we were determined enough and we were right. We rewrote management education in this country. A generation of managers was affected for the better.

'And yet, in the end, it just faded. The dream died. Paul moved on, we all got older. Somehow it just didn't seem so important any more. Maybe we're the reactionaries now....'

DISCUSSION

The revolutionaries of yesterday are the reactionaries of today. The revolutionaries of today are the reactionaries of tomorrow. People are children of their time. However alert one is to the shortcomings of a previous age, it's rare to preserve such perspicacity when it's your time, your traditions which are in question.

In this case, a cadre of committed people has determinedly set out to change the status quo. Their subculture has successfully challenged the prevailing culture. And because their subculture has delivered better results, it has triumphed.

But mistakes have been made. How has the bubble of subculture been viewed by people outside it? What negative forces have been unleashed by these middle-aged, once angry men? Might evolution, not revolution, have been a better policy? Revolutions tend to have bad track records....

The harbingers of change have come from the same age group and background. As a cohort group, they have aged together – seemingly with little notion of succession or renewal. Dependence upon the presence of a charismatic leader has exacerbated these weaknesses. Initiators of change, like good managers everywhere, should act to make themselves dispensable. They must positively seek out their successors.

Typically, culture change is thought of in terms of no more than a few years. While dramatic cultural shifts can be achieved in this timeframe, merely to think in terms of a few years is myopic. Culture change is, above all, a political process, and some political processes are unending.

Again, change is often construed as being discrete, a one-off occurrence. But the notion that organizations can somehow be put right is a startlingly naive one, a sort of medical metaphor of a company doctor performing surgery on a tumour.

Organizations must be effective in their responses to the environment. Today's economic and political environment is in a state of flux where, as Heraclitus once remarked, the only constant is change itself. Organizational change must be a dynamic, never-ending process of evolution where the dinosaur award goes to those who stand still long enough.

Those who initiate change must create infrastructures by which the change process of adaptation, survival and success may be perpetuated. Often this means the original pioneers standing aside as their ideas and influence become redundant, if not thoroughly counterproductive. In the long term, they may be more respected for giving away power than hanging on to it. They will certainly be behaving more responsibly.

KEY POINTS

- ○   Change is a dynamic act of adaptation essential for the perpetuation of life itself.
- ○   Evolutionary change is almost always better than revolutionary change.
- ○   Change is a political process; like all political processes, it must be well managed.
- ○   Inspirers of change must always be aware of the dangers of short-termism and the possible limitations of their thought.
- ○   There is a time to take power and a time to relinquish it. These times should not be confused.

PRINCIPLE

Change will require renewal. Prepare for it.

PART IV

SUCCESSFUL CULTURE CHANGE

❖

AN EXAMPLE OF LEARNING

When I was very young I taught myself to ride a bike by the simple expedient of surreptitiously abstracting one from its environment and getting on it. A good heave got me started. The bike was far too big for me but I ignored that and simply pedalled away, for all I was worth. Obediently, the bike wobbled off down the road. Hurrah! I was in business....

Not for long, however. Encountering my first bend, the wobble turned into a pronounced tilt. I tried to rectify it but to no avail. To my dismay, the bike tottered drunkenly and keeled over into the ditch, taking me with it. As I recall, there was an almighty crash.

At this point I had a choice. One option was clearly to give up and write off cycling as a nasty experience. If I did that, then all I would learn about cycling would be to avoid it – although I would begin to learn about failure. A second option was to get back on the bike and strive to repeat the experience – probably with the same results. Again, I would be learning nothing more about cycling, although I would be learning about persistence. The third option was to find out what the hell had happened – so that I could ensure it wouldn't happen again.

Instinctively I chose the latter option. I knew nothing about centres of gravity but I postulated a wobble factor. The bike had wobbled on the straight; this had involved loss of control. However, wobbling around bends seemed to involve further loss of control to the point of a crash. Ergo – wobble less on bends. How do I do that? Hold on tight to the handlebars and pedal faster. This took some nerve for I was now risking a much worse crash, but I quickly found that it worked. As Nietzsche said, 'He who survives is in the right.'

Thus emboldened, I headed forth into a childhood full of crashes, bruises and scrapes of every hue and description.

A MODEL OF LEARNING

In the example above, I learned to ride a bike – no great feat in itself but interesting as an early experience of learning. What had I done? Unwittingly, I had followed the learning cycle shown in Figure 14.

This learning cycle is based upon the work of the psychologists Piaget and Kolb. Let's follow it and see how it does justice to my experience of learning to ride a bike.

I started with **behaviour**. I did something – rode the bike. This led to a **result** – ending up in the ditch. If I had abandoned all further notions of riding a bike then I would have advanced no further on this cycle. If I had simply repeated the experience, then the result would, most likely, have been replicated. Again, I would not have advanced. I would have been trapped in my experience.

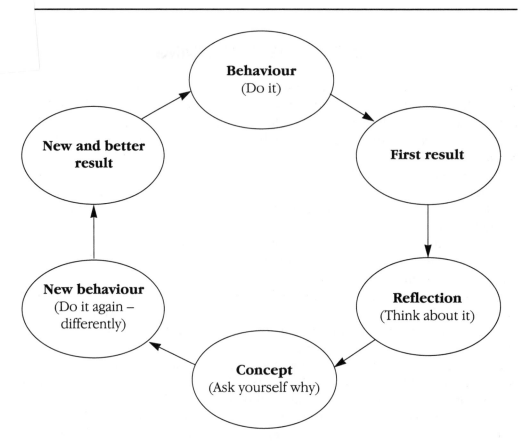

FIGURE 14   LEARNING FROM EXPERIENCE

To progress further – to learn to learn – I had to move to the next stage of learning which was **reflection** – sitting in the ditch thinking about what happened – as we would say today, replaying the video. This stage is a necesary precursor to the vital third stage – developing a **concept** or concepts to explain what happened. Armed with concepts, one can hypothesize and experiment; without concepts, we are trapped in our experience. In my case, the concept was a crude wobble factor. But, crude or not, it worked.

My **new behaviour** led to a **new and better result**. Now, I could directly compare the new result with the old one. Successfully rounding the bend was immeasurably more fulfilling than miserably ending up in the ditch. Naturally, the new behaviour was quickly conditioned so that, in no time, I was whizzing around bends at high speed with nary a wobble.

So the learning cycle works. The learning cycle is itself a concept, a model of learning. Many managers are deeply suspicious of concepts. Their educations may, as mine once was, have been in so-called 'hard' subjects such as accountancy or engineering. They may have images of themselves as practical people with no time for mere theorizing. And, not least, they may have had bad experiences of conceptual sleight of hand. But not to have concepts is to remain trapped in experience. And to remain trapped in experience is to learn nothing. If we learn nothing, then we are condemned endlessly to repeat the same mistakes while simultaneously lagging further and further behind as the world changes around us. Learning is vital to our survival, as individuals, groups, organizations, even species. Concepts are the prime instruments of learning; with them we can structure knowledge from raw experience. We should treasure concepts because of their power to help us learn. And one of the most fundamental and useful of concepts is the one above which gives us a model of learning itself.

LEARNING FROM EXPERIENCE

When you were at school, most of your learning was by instruction, but the really important lessons in life are learned through personal experience – losing your virginity, falling in love, seeing your mother die, holding your newborn baby in your arms. Learning here was with the most precious currency of all – your personal experience, your sweat and tears. The real lessons in life are not learned at normal school; they are learned in what Frank Sinatra laughingly calls the school of hard knocks.

Management is nothing if not pragmatic. Managers, thus, are arch-pragmatists – because they need to be. Although many managers think of learning in terms of instruction, ironically, most managers learn best from experience. Case studies are vicarious experience, as close to the real thing as you can get. And, of course, far more is learned from failure than success. Success tells us only that we have succeeded; it doesn't necessarily tell us why. (Countless entrepreneurs have succeeded, in spite of themselves, only to lose all in harsher trading conditions.) But to try, fail, learn and then succeed, that is learning!

This book has one purpose: to aid your learning. The case studies are vicarious experience. They deal with failure because most change initiatives do fail, and because we learn best and most from failure, painful though it undoubtedly is. The concepts which I introduce are to help you make sense of your real and vicarious experience of change so that you use a different approach in future and gain better results.

Let's briefly review our vicarious experience and, at least, learn what not to do.

THE LESSONS OF METHODOLOGY

The principles derived from the relevant case studies are as follows:

're getting ready to get ready...'
crastination and change
crastination is a waste of everyone's time.

'Just stirring things up...'
Provocation and change
Seeking to provoke change is unprofessional, irresponsible and counterproductive.

'We bought the dream...'
Realistic change
Change objectives must be realistic.

'It's divergent...'
Focused change
Change must ultimately focus upon improved results.

'It's going to be top-down...'
Top-down change
Change needs to be both top-down and bottom-up.

'It's bottom-up...'
Bottom-up change
Change needs to be both bottom-up and top-down.

'We need an attitude change around here!'
Attitude change
Trying to change behaviour by changing attitude is approaching the problem from the wrong direction. It will fail.

'One hell of a culture problem...'
Culture change
Trying to change behaviour by changing culture is approaching the problem from the wrong direction. It will fail.

'We got the package'
Packaged change
Packaged solutions don't work.

'We've tried it...'
Experimenting with change
With change, don't try it. Do it.

'We're doing it ourselves...'
DIY change
DIY culture change doesn't work. It can't.

'We've got these hot-shot consultants'
Consultancy and change
Process consultancy is vital for culture change.

'We've got too much change!'
Too much change
People's capacity to handle change is potentially infinite.

Put like this, the principles appear disarmingly simplistic. In every case, however, they were drawn from change experiences which had gone awry. All of the blunders could have been avoided by learning about change before embarking upon it. The arrogant will remain unconvinced and mutter, 'It's only common sense.' To which I would reply – common sense is notoriously uncommon. By avoiding such bear traps, you would be doing better than hundreds of organizations which have spent millions of pounds in futile and misguided change imperatives.

THE LESSONS OF IMPLEMENTATION

The principles derived from the relevant case studies are as follows:

'We're traumatized...'
People and change
Successful change requires superlative people skills.

'Get your tanks off my lawn...'
Resistance and change
Much of the challenge of successfully managing change lies in helping people overcome their resistance to it.

'It's industrial anarchy...'
Openness and change
Tactical openness is almost always necessary for successful change.

'We told them all right – we just didn't communicate...'
Communication and change
Successful change requires superlative communication.

'These aren't any measurable improvements...'
Results and change
Change without results is no change at all.

'Things are getting worse, not better...'
Performance and change
Performance drops with change; with successful change, it dramatically improves.

'We declared UDI...'
Politics and change
Management is political; change is much more so.

'Somebody mugged our baby...'
More politics and change
Management is political; change is much, much more so.

'We've restructured...'
Structure and change
True change is about reprocessing (new behaviour), rather than merely restructuring (different jobs)

'You don't know shit from Shinola!'
Information and change
The right change requires the right information for the right people at the right time.

'The strategy was great, but...'
Mechanisms for change
Change requires well-considered, integrated enabling mechanisms.

'They talk a good fight...'
Project management and change
Change requires superlative project management.

'We just ran out of steam...'
Change and renewal
Change will require renewal. Prepare for it.

Again the principles appear simple. Like the wheel, or gravity, or the benzene ring structure, they are simple in retrospect. If I set out to learn the piano by myself, I would make lots of mistakes. Similarly, these are the sort of mistakes which organizations make when learning about change. Arrogance is the root cause of every one of them, arrogance which states that the natural world is a serious subject for study (physics, engineering) but that the social world is an area about which everybody mysteriously just knows.

It's worth noting that, although these lessons are simple enough, they are also difficult. How can this be? Saying that superlative people skills are necessary for change is simple. Actually developing and correctly deploying such skills is extremely difficult. How many managers have superlative people skills? Very, very few, and if you still talk about 'man management' then it's a surety that your people skills fall well short. Even if you have such skills, a change project will leave you drained and haggard with the effort of resolving people issues.

A CRITICAL NOTE

To date, we have largely been dealing with what goes wrong, because, empirically, most change initiatives do go wrong. We have indentified many of the more common factors which, singly or in unison, scupper change. There are undoubtedly other factors which we have not identified.

But in the exercises of working through what goes wrong, we have probably become much more aware of the sort of clues and signs for which to watch out. Obviously it's far better to note problems in the methodological stage rather than the implementation stage. Skilful professionals in the discipline of change develop an almost uncanny sixth sense for the right and wrong paths to follow.

The downside is that we've been working through negatives. Sorry! And we need to recognize that not acting wrongly will not guarantee that we are acting correctly. In other words, not making the mistakes listed above will not necessarily lead to a successful change project. What we need to do now is return to the original problems of culture and change with the eyes of experience and consider what sort of approach needs to be taken.

AN EXAMPLE OF CULTURE CHANGE

Let's go back to where we started – with Fernando and Thor. They found they simply couldn't work together; thus it was inferred that their companies couldn't work together. Consequently, their proposed joint venture was indefinitely postponed and their strategic alliance never happened.

Both companies accepted this state of affairs. In effect, the Trolltind/Ibanez bicycle had landed in the ditch with a resounding crash. And because both companies accepted such a dismal state of affairs, no more was going to be learned about joint ventures; people were only going to learn about failure.

But let's suppose someone in, say, Trolltind, simply hadn't accepted this state of affairs. Suppose they argued that abandoning joint ventures and possible alliances because of personal incompatibility just wasn't good enough. Suppose they said, 'This is crazy. If senior managers in our respective companies can't work together, we've got a real problem – and one which we need to sort out right now. Both companies need their people to work with such outsiders. If we have to abandon this joint venture, then let's do so for a good reason. This is not a good reason.'

Suppose they contacted someone in Ibanez and talked the problem through with them until they had reached mutual agreement. Suppose they then (and this is by fax and phone, remember, with no body distance) said, 'Well, *we* seem to be able to work together, so why the hell can't our people?' Suppose they agreed that they would send Thor and Fernando back to the negotiating table but, this time, they would have an Organization Development (OD) consultant with them.

Two weeks later, Thor and Fernando reluctantly sat down in a rented conference room in Great Dunmow, Essex. With them was their OD consultant, who, as it happened, did not work for either Trolltind or Ibanez.

Although Fernando and Thor tried their utmost to get down to business, if only out of professional pique, soon they got caught up once more in their vicious spiral. This time, however, it was even worse. (Once you start to learn about failure, each bad experience sets you up for the next one.) Quite soon, they were at each other's throats.

Choking off an expletive because there was a woman in the room, Fernando looked across at Carla, their OD consultant. 'What the hell are you here for anyway?' he demanded. 'And why don't you stop this – this farce?' 'Yes, why are you here?' Thor concurred.

'To answer your second question first – I have no mandate to, as you say, stop this farce,' Carla replied. 'Anyway, don't you think that it's rather unbecoming for you to be engaged in such a farce?' she added. Without waiting for his reply, she continued. 'Do you realize that you have both agreed on something? You want to know why I am here. But you already know why I am here.' She gestured towards a fax on the table and quoted verbatim, '"to assist in the resolution of interpersonal differences...". That, gentlemen, is why I am here.'

'And how do you propose to do that?' Thor queried, intrigued by her calmness. Carla stared levelly at him. 'First, by agreeing a contract with both of you.' 'A contract?' Fernando said. 'You mean a legal contract?' 'No, Fernando,' Carla told him. 'A psychological contract.

'You are grown men behaving like boys. You are senior managers, behaving in a thoroughly unprofessional manner. This has grave consequences for both of your companies. Both of your companies have asked you to come back to try again – and succeed this time. I am here to help you do this. But I cannot help you unless all three of us agree that we will work together to resolve these differences.' She paused and looked unwaveringly at each of them with calm, grey eyes. 'That is what I mean by a psychological contract. It is not to do with law; it is to do with integrity.'

Thor stared at her. 'I do not know what you can do but, for my part, I am willing to enter into this, what do you call it, this psychological contract.' He glanced at Fernando. 'All right then; me too.' Carla surveyed them. 'Good. This is the first stage.

We are agreed that you have a problem in working together. And we are agreed that all of us will work on this problem. Let us now do so.' 'One question, Carla,' Thor said. 'Why did you not make this clear at the beginning?' Again, Carla gestured towards the fax. 'It was clear at the beginning. But you were not looking at it. You were too busy fighting your personal war. So my mandate had to come direct from the rigours of war. There was no other way.' Thor nodded thoughtfully.

In the following days, Carla fed back to them their stereotypes of each other. 'Fernando, the fiery Latin, Thor, the gloomy Scandinavian. This is soap opera, I think. Perhaps we need Carla, the Italian, singing an aria?' At this, they looked at her shame-facedly.

Working back from stereotypes to first impressions, she quickly pinpointed body distance. 'My goodness, so that's all it was,' Thor exclaimed. 'Yes and no,' Carla replied. 'Body distance, it would appear, became your cause of war. But if it had not been body distance, it would probably have been something else. The real power at work was the power of culture, of which both of you were unaware.'

Carla explained how culture is formed, using the same model which we developed in Part I (illustrated by Figures 1, 2 and 3 which are shown again here). She explained the difficulty in moving beyond our cultural frames of reference. She explained the importance of so doing by what she called 'the management of difference'.

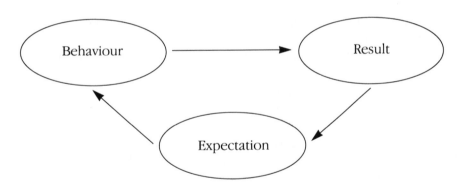

FIGURE 1   THE DEVELOPMENT OF EXPECTATION

'A great deal of human behaviour is tribal. We most easily relate to people from the same background, the same sort of school, the same social class. But if we do not take great care, we live in cultural prisons. We do not realize they are prisons because we can see out; but we cannot see the glass which prevents us getting out.

'Today we can no longer afford to live in cultural prisons. Business is truly international, polycultural, multilingual. Look at us three ... Fernando, you are Spanish, working for a Spanish company. Thor, you are a Dane, working for a Norwegian

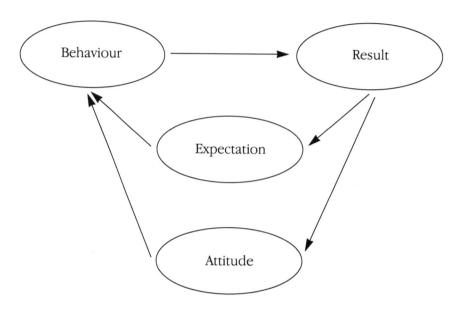

FIGURE 2 THE DEVELOPMENT OF ATTITUDE

company. I am an Italian, working for a French company.' She laughed. 'And here we are, in Essex, England.

'We must learn to work with people who are very different from us. We must learn about cultural influences and imperatives – ours and theirs. We must learn to change our behaviour, our expectations, and, in time, our attitudes and culture, if it is necessary. We must learn about change. We must learn to learn.'

She looked at them. 'Otherwise, we remain as frightened little boys, throwing stones.' Fernando and Thor glanced at each other, abashed.

Carla was present at all of their meetings that summer. Thor looked back on their time in Apt, Orleans and Dublin with a sort of stunned amazement. 'I never knew how much there was to learn,' Thor admitted, 'about myself, about other people.' He wrote a paper on the need for what he called 'cultural renegotiation' and presented it to the president of Trolltind. It came as no surprise to find that Fernando had suggested a similar initiative in Ibanez. On the day when the contract for the Trolltind/Ibanez joint venture was signed, Thor clinked champagne glasses with Carla on the terrace at Berne. 'So, now we have a legal contract, not just a psychological one,' he joked. Carla nodded, looking thoughtfully at him. 'I think you have developed a taste for learning, Thor, for personal discovery. You will be following the learning cycle for many a long year to come.'

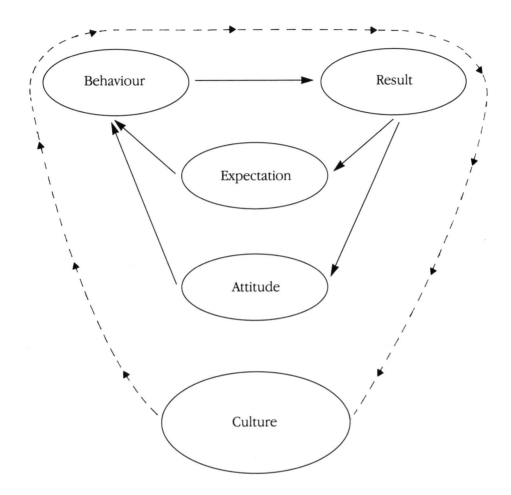

FIGURE 3 THE DEVELOPMENT OF CULTURE

A MODEL OF CULTURE CHANGE

In helping Thor and Fernando to escape from their cultural prisons and manage their differences, what, in essence, has Carla done? She has taken them along a learning cycle such as that shown in Figure 14. Thor and Fernando have been learning from experience; Carla's role has been to enable them to learn from experience.

The learning cycle which Carla initiated and which Thor and Fernando followed is shown in Figure 15. Let us examine each stage in turn.

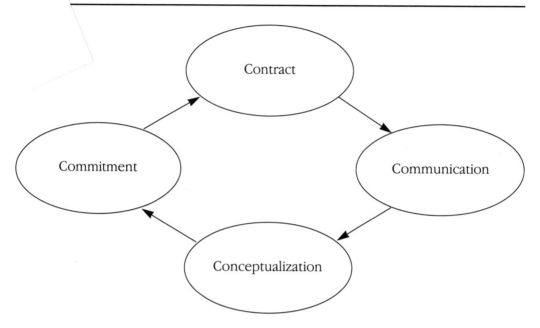

FIGURE 15   A MODEL OF CULTURE CHANGE

THE CONTRACT

Thor and Fernando had a problem. They knew that they had a problem but they would not face up to it. In what has become somewhat of a cliché, they did not have **ownership** of it. Carla could not help them until they accepted ownership of their problem, and became committed to working at it to effect a resolution and to accepting her help.

The example of Thor, Fernando and Carla is highly abbreviated. Moving through any of the stages of this culture change cycle is a fraught affair – even with two people. Without a suitable contract – psychological, not legal – they would have lacked the integrity of commitment. When their relationship became fraught and the going got tough, they would have relapsed into blame, attacked Carla, in fact, done anything to obscure the issue.

Without a contract, people will not properly commit to change. Building a change programme without a contract is like building a house without foundations. It will not stand.

COMMUNICATION

The next stage was undoubtedly communication. Both Thor and Fernando had to say how they saw each other and how they thought the other saw them. They even had to suggest why their opposite number might see them in this light. Carla had to make both of them understand that blame must be suspended. She had to enable them to investigate their perceptions. Fernando saw Thor as cold and aloof. Fair enough; no judgement needed. But what *specifically* did Thor do which was so cold and aloof? Fernando started to realize that, no matter what Thor actually did, he would still be – unfairly – seen as cold and aloof. Thus Fernando had to confront his own biases. Carla had to lead them painstakingly through a process of mutual discovery – about perceptions, stereotypes, behaviour, outcomes, expectations, attitudes, culture. They needed to watch a video in which they were the principal players. They had to learn to see themselves as they were, not as they liked to imagine. They needed to see how their cultural norms were creating an untenable business situation. Painful stuff. Nearly all of us go through life swathed in a cocoon of illusion, insulated from reality. Why? Because reality is painful. The reality about ourselves can be extremely painful and threatening to our psyches. But, as Carla patiently enabled Thor and Fernando to realize, managers are paid to manage reality, not illusion. Much of the insulation has to be stripped away.

CONCEPTUALIZATION

The third stage, which overlaps the second stage, is generating concepts. It's not enough just to watch the video in the second stage. One must understand the video. Understanding the video requires concepts. A large part of Carla's job was to provide suitable concepts.

Carla came armed with hundreds of concepts. Thor and Fernando were oblivious to this because the concepts were all in her mind. Both Thor and Fernando had participated in dozens of training and management development seminars over the years. Consequently, they viewed facilitators as people handing out sheaves of case studies, psychometric tests, etc. All Carla had was a flip chart and a couple of pens which anybody could use. But, time and time again, she produced exactly the right concept at exactly the right moment for one or other of them to understand part of their 'cultural mosaic', as Thor laughingly called it. Carla demonstrated that trying to change without using appropriate concepts is like trying to build a house without bricks.

COMMITMENT

Carla repeatedly emphasized that conceptual understanding, while fundamental, was still passive with regard to change. 'You can understand what's wrong; you can understand what needs to be done. But until you're actually doing it, day in and day out, how can you say that you've changed?' To this, Thor and Fernando could only acquiesce.

Change occurs only when something different happens – and continues to happen. It was not sufficient for Fernando and Thor to agree to have a better relationship; they had to pinpoint specific areas where they were going to behave differently. And then they had to commit to actually behaving differently. Many of these areas concerned elements of behaviour which they had previously taken for granted. Fernando, for instance, to his great chagrin, had to learn to listen and not to interrupt. Repeatedly, Carla tripped him up by demonstrating that he didn't know what Thor had just said because he hadn't been listening. Instead, he had been busy preparing his next interruption. Thor had to learn to focus on specific outcomes and not to be sidetracked by secondary issues. He had to learn always to check on progress – his own and other people's – and on mutual understanding. 'I have had to learn all those things which I took for granted,' he ruefully confessed to Carla. 'That's what culture change is all about,' she replied, 'challenging your taken for granteds.'

Movement around this learning cycle was not regular or uniform. For any one cultural variable, there might be overlapping of stages, for example between communication and conceptualization. Movement might also be iterative; it might go from communication to conceptualization, back to communication and forward again to conceptualization. Experiential learning does not proceed along a smooth curve; very often, it proceeds in fits and starts. Clearly, however, the contract phase involves a definite commitment to proceed with a process of problem resolution. And the commitment phase involves an act of integrity – that we will proceed with this course of action (i.e. behaviour) rather than any other. So contract and commitment are sharper, more precise than communication and conceptualization. Iteration here is apt to be backsliding!

It's worth specifying exactly what I mean by commitment. I do not mean agreement. Agreement is passive. Each day, at work, people agree to all sorts of proposals which they have no intention of ever fulfilling – unrealistic corporate objectives, hockey stick sales curves, mysterious recoveries which always seem to occur in the third quarter. After years in management, one quite simply grows tired of listening to such agreements. The people making them feel good about themselves ('Look at what I've just agreed to!') or they feel momentary relief ('I'm off the hook'). By the inevitable day of reckoning, however, a host of convenient excuses has come to mind. Such agreements are worthless; all they do is graphically demonstrate the utter lack of integrity of those making them.

This argument is even more applicable when it comes to change. Politically, an easy way to fend off change is to agree to everything and covertly ensure that convenient factors (beyond your control, of course) frustrate events – meanwhile doing everything in your power to ensure that the initiators of change are discredited and run out of time. For obvious reasons, I call this 'boxing to be saved by the bell'. It is a common ploy among senior managers who, politically, must be seen to be in favour of change but are secretly against it.

This type of spurious agreement can be used to con other people, or it can be used to con yourself. Either way, it's worthless. So how does one know whether an agreement is spurious? One doesn't.

My definition of **commitment** is this: **if you commit to something then you do it**. No excuses; no rationalizations. It is an act of integrity, of honour. If you say you'll do it then you do.

On this basis, commitment can only be assessed retrospectively. You would only know that someone had committed to something when it had actually been achieved. In practice, that doesn't matter. Agreement is a passive, mild statement of intent. Commitment is an active, strong statement of intention. With agreement, failure involves little loss. With commitment, failure involves loss of integrity. The contract of commitment is a thousand times more powerful than the contract of agreement.

Without commitment, people will not change. The currency of change is not words (necessary though they undoubtedly are); the currency of change is action and progress.

You may be sure that, before she was finished, Carla ensured that her two protégés were well aware of the significance of this distinction.

CONFLICT: THE IMPORTANCE OF ASSERTIVENESS

My whole approach to culture change rests on the premise that it must and can be managed to a significant degree. The cycle of culture change discussed in the last section gives us a model and a mechanism for such change. Underlying this model and mechanism, however, is an approach to problem resolution which says that without assertiveness no problem will truly be resolved.

What do we mean by this? Well, originally, Thor and Fernando were in a state of conflict – escalating conflict at that. We are all aware of how trivial issues can blow up into arguments of alarming proportions. The power of emotion often ensures that two people, who were only slightly apart, rapidly become alienated and finish miles away from each other. That was exactly what happened to Thor and Fernando.

Conflict is a natural and inevitable feature of human interaction. All human beings are, to some extent, similar; and all human beings are, to some extent, different. Our similarity is rarely problematic; our difference usually is. Unless we manage our differences, our differences will manage us. Finally, conflict will manage us.

In any conflict between two people (for example, Thor and Fernando), there are four possible outcomes:

1.   I win; you lose.
2.   I lose; you win.
3.   I lose; you lose.
4.   We win.

A little thought reveals that outcome 1 will probably lead to outcome 2 next time (as you exact your revenge) and thus outcome 3 will be the final result. Similarly, outcome 2 will tend to lead to outcome 1 and thus, finally, to outcome 3.

The stark reality of conflict is that everyone loses. Nowhere is this more vividly seen than in war – conflict brought to its natural conclusion. Neither Thor nor Fernando were happy with their conflict; both were prisoners of it.

Until Carla's intervention, Thor and Fernando had defined their conflict in interpersonal terms. It was 'all the other guy's fault' – the characteristic sign of interpersonal conflict. This is shown in Figure 16. By securing the first, crucial contract from both of them, Carla managed to change the situation from Figure 16 to Figure 17.

FIGURE 16   INTERPERSONAL CONFLICT

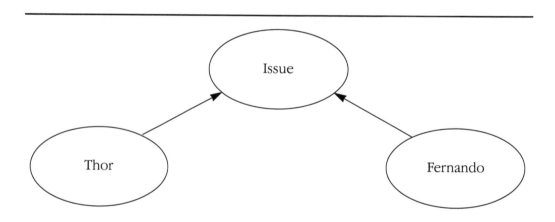

FIGURE 17   ASSERTIVENESS AND ISSUE RESOLUTION

Note that in Figure 17 I am using the neutral term 'issue' for what was undoubtedly a problem for both protagonists. Sometimes an issue will be a problem for only one protagonist, but the issue will be recognizable to both. Also, the word 'issue' is much less emotive than the word 'problem'. In moving away from interpersonal conflict, we must learn to lay aside our emotion, to become dispassionate.

There are three elements to this change in focus:

1.   Mutual respect

I respect myself and I respect you. Therefore I will not attempt to attack or manipulate you. I ask you to behave likewise.

2.   Legitimate disagreement

Nevertheless, we have an issue about which we disagree. Irrespective of which (if either) of us is wrong or right, we still have a disagreement. Everybody has their right to their own viewpoint and we are all sometimes right and sometimes wrong. So our disagreement is quite legitimate. However, it is not helpful or desirable.

3.   Psychological contract

I commit to working with you on this issue so that we can arrive at a mutually accept-able and beneficial outcome.

Obviously both parties must progress through these stages. There needs to be joint commitment. Only then will outcome 3 of the conflict (I lose; you lose) be exchanged for outcome 4 (we win).

There is a plethora of books about assertiveness, almost all dealing with it at the level of method, of technique. For precisely this reason, it seems inappropriate to enter into specific techniques here. It is important, though, to appreciate the value of assertiveness at the level of methodology. Conflict is about attacking people; assertive-ness is about resolving issues. Whatever the techniques being employed, people always know whether they're in conflict mode or assertiveness mode. Change initia-tives, by their very nature, involve conflict – conflict of histories, experiences, norms, values, perceptions, actions. If people do not rapidly adopt the assertiveness mode, they will wallow and drown in politics and infighting.

CULTURE CHANGE IN ORGANIZATIONS

The model of culture change developed in the previous sections came from the expe-riences of two individuals who faced issues of culture and change. Is it therefore applicable to whole organizations facing such change? The model is, indeed, equally applicable, but the difficulty of applying it is far greater. As Carla would be the first to admit, it's akin to the difference between playing chess and playing three-dimensional chess.

In Part I (see p. 24) we discussed the social reality of organizations, how organiza-tional life truly is, as distinct from how we like to think about it. Organizations are composed of people and people are very bad at facing up to reality because, as we have noted in the discussion concerning Thor and Fernando, it hurts. People avoid reality, the issues which they know deep down that they should face, by attacking other people, not by resolving such issues. When the issues are themselves interper-sonal, it's even worse. People will say, 'I've got a real problem with that lot. They just never deliver.' But they rarely face up to the issue, because they don't want to risk psychic hurt. Instead, they vicariously attack by endless complaining about the opposition. Griping lowers their anxiety level, but it is coping, not resolution.

Management necessitates dealing with reality, resolving issues, not just coping with them. Do managers truly achieve this? Rarely. At the social level, most organizations are mouldering collections of unresolved issues which have been endlessly recycled. Interpersonal relationships are partial at best, blocked at worst. Everybody knows about it; everybody lives with it.

The miracle with such blockage is that organizations manage to function at all. But such blockage hardly enhances their functioning. By the time we've finished with personal rivalries, interdepartmental conflict and office politics, it's suprising that anything is ever achieved.

Change raises the ante. Suddenly all the creepy-crawlies that are hiding under dark stones start to encounter daylight as the stones roll back. This can be very threatening. I once worked on a process chemical industry site where two key workers, occupying a control room on the night shift, had not spoken to each other for the previous fourteen years. Neither of them could even remember what the original disagreement was about. Certainly they had never made a contract, psychological or otherwise, to work on their problem. Everybody knew about this potentially lethal threat to safety in a plant which was physically highly intimidating; no one, for fourteen years, had faced up to it.

Culture change in organizations involves replacing dysfunctional behaviour with functional behaviour – and making sure that the functional behaviour remains. The dysfunctional behaviour might or might not have been functional once, but it is now dysfunctional. In basic terms we are returning to the situation outlined in Figure 3 and renegotiating it. Figure 3 is reproduced here as Figure 18.

By progressing through the contract, communication, conceptualization, commitment cycle, people are helped to understand the power of attitude and culture, the lead time of change and the necessity of change. They are further helped to make specific behavioural change which is permanent.

In an organization, this is extremely difficult. Change is happening at an individual level, at a group level, and at an organizational level. Any issue which will imperil change must be dealt with in a timely fashion; the longer it remains, the more the atmosphere will be poisoned.

The notion that people in an organization can somehow continue running their day-to-day business while changing themselves is naive. It assumes that no skill is required in managing change, yet experience suggests otherwise. Running the business (or other activity) is a full-time effort. Acquiring change is also a full-time effort. Although the same people are involved in both efforts (they have to be) the notion that the same people can direct both efforts is absurd.

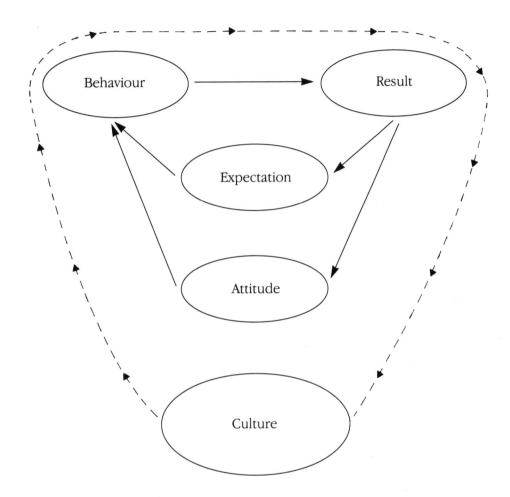

FIGURE 18   THE DEVELOPMENT OF CULTURE

CONSULTANCY ROLES

People commonly think of consultants as professional advisers. Certainly when we consult a doctor or a solicitor we expect professional advice. The role of a consultant – any consultant – is to help us resolve problems. This may, or may not, involve advice.

Let's imagine I have a problem with the plumbing in my house. I poke and fiddle around with a stick but to no avail. So I phone a plumber. Along she comes and asks me what seems to be the problem. Dutifully I tell her that the drains are blocked. At this point (it is tacitly assumed) I hand the problem over to her. She is the expert and she will solve it. Happily she does so and the drains are soon unblocked.

I have consulted a plumber. I have bought expertise. I have passed the problem over to an expert and the expert has passed the solution back to me. The expert has, unsurprisingly, acted in expert role.

Now let's consider another scenario. This time, I have a very different kind of problem, a personal problem in my marriage. Again I try to solve it. Metaphorically, I poke and fiddle about with a stick – but again to no avail. So again I seek consultation. I visit a marriage guidance counsellor.

Again, I have bought expertise – but expertise of a different kind. When I ask the counsellor for a solution, she tells me that giving me a solution (advice) is not appropriate. At this, I grow somewhat offended and ask her to explain. Patiently, she does. She explains that my plumbing problem was a technical problem which I could reasonably delegate to a responsible expert – who would then deliver the solution. But my marriage problem is not a technical problem in the same way. It is not something which I can delegate to another person because change, if it is needed, will not be change for my plumbing system, it will be change for me.

This is why my marriage counsellor will not give me a solution. Giving me a solution will not enable me to change. And let's say, in order to solve this problem in my marriage, I do have to change. So, unlike the plumber, she cannot function as my technical expert. My problem is too personal and fundamental to be delegated to anyone else. If it involves me changing, then I must be responsible for such change; I have to make the change and I will have to live with it.

My counsellor is not prepared to function as an expert. She is prepared to function as a facilitator. What does that mean? It means that she will do her utmost to help me find and implement a solution – my own solution.

Broadly speaking, there are two management consultancy roles, corresponding to the roles of plumber and marriage counsellor respectively. The first is the **expert** role – the specialist who fixes our computer or notifies us of changes in legislation. The second is the **process** or **facilitatory** role – the generalist who helps us to resolve difficult issues. The use of the word **process** means that, in this case, a **process consultant** helps us with our processes – of thinking, feeling, learning, developing – in the same way in which Carla helped Thor and Fernando. She didn't give them solutions; she helped them develop solutions.

Managers are very familiar with the expert role. Organizations are, after all, structured in terms of expert role. Sales people deal with sales; they do not deal with production. Managers think in terms of specialisms – an expert in computers or legislation. They think in terms of boxes of skills which they may need.

Traditionally, many management consultancies have operated along similar lines. They have been collectives of specialisms – experts in production, experts in marketing, experts in psychology. And they have sold functionally expert solutions – in other words, packages.

The trouble is twofold. The notion that packages are somehow appropriate for client problems from Hartlepool to Helsinki is a curious one. Reality suggests otherwise. And, irrespective of appropriateness, packages will always be seen as external and imposed; they will thus be resisted by the people who need to change. As we saw in the case study 'We got the package' in Part II, packages simply do not work.

For change management, the expert role does not work either. It is of little use writing reports full of recommendations (solutions) to clients. It is extremely rare for such recommendations to be implemented and even if they are implemented, the real effort is not diagnosis but implementation (change) itself.

The process role is the prime consultancy role for change management. A process consultant has to help his or her clients diagnose the need for change, what that change should be and how it should occur. Furthermore, the consultant should remain with the clients until such change has been realized. An expert consultant can make a recommendation and walk away from it; a process consultant can't.

Many managers on their first contact with process consultancy find it extremely strange. Is it all a confidence trick? Can anyone do it? What skills, if any, are required? Is there any guarantee that it will work? As with Thor, Fernando and Carla, there is a mutual learning curve to experience.

Both expert and process consultants make use of expertise. Expert consultants give advice; process consultants do not. People will act on advice on specific, technical matters, but advice will not change people. If you advise a friend who has a drinking problem to give up alcohol, will they? I think not. Only facilitation has any chance.

In the course of a change project, the consultancy role may change from process to expert and back to process again. As I made clear in the case study 'We've got these hot-shot consultants' in Part II, it is essential that, at any time, both clients and consultants know which role they are occupying and why they are occupying it.

People think of process consultancy as something very new. In truth, it is not. In terms of rational argument, Socrates was probably the greatest process consultant the world has ever seen. He didn't tell people they were right or wrong. He helped them to discover for themselves whether they were right or wrong.

Although process consultancy seems 'softer' than expert consultancy, in truth it is harder. With culture change programmes, a process consultant must be hypersensitive to what is happening, to what has happened in the past and to what is likely to happen. They must be possessed of almost uncanny powers of perception.

To say that anyone can be a process consultant is akin to suggesting that anyone can write poetry. Yes, just about anyone can write bad poetry. In any country, there are probably no more than a few dozen outstanding poets living at any one time. Similarly, there are probably no more than a few dozen first-rate process consultants living at any one time. It's that hard.

In no way do I wish to diminish the value of the expert role. It has its necessary place (a surgeon performing an operation, a barrister preparing a case). But it is inappropriate for facilitating change. As the case study made clear (see p. 65 'We've got these hot-shot consultants'), change which is expert-driven is consultant-driven and will fail. While the expert role and the process role are both consultative, they are consultative in completely different meanings of the word.

For completeness, it is probably best to mention here two other roles which sometimes add to the general confusion. These are the **locum manager** role and the **company doctor** role.

Consultants acting in either expert or process role have no management authority whatsoever. They are there to help managers, and performing managers' jobs for them is emphatically not helping them. Rather it is weakening them. Process consultants, in particular, tend to be acutely aware of this. At each attempt by a client to pass the buck, the buck must be politely passed back again. Equally, process consultants must be permanently alert for the client becoming dependent upon them. The phenomenon of **transference** (client/consultant dependence) is commonly understood in clinical situations; it is just as prevalent in work situations. If you are engendering dependence in your clients, then either you are manipulating them or they are manipulating you, or both. Whichever is the case, they are being done a disservice.

Consultants acting in expert role are often drawn into taking over management functions. Because their expertise is in the content of their specialism (MRPII, psychometrics) rather than the process of consulting itself, they find it extraordinarily difficult to resist. But they must resist.

The other two roles mentioned do, quite legitimately, employ management authority. A locum manager is simply someone brought in from outside temporarily to occupy a managerial post. Whether or not they have come from a consultancy, that is their role. If they try to be clever and combine the roles of manager and management consultant, most likely, they will spectacularly fail. The roles and commitments are different.

A company doctor is someone who comes in to occupy the chief executive role and run the company. Company doctors tend to operate in company turnaround situations which call for sharp, painful 'surgery'. They are thus a particular type of locum manager. In the past, the management consultant role was often confused with the company doctor role. They are quite separate.

In summary, for corporate culture change you need a process consultant. Do not make the mistake of trying to do it all yourself (DIY change) and do not make the mistake of trying to get other people to do it for you (consultant-driven change). Enlist someone who understands culture, change and consultancy.

ORGANIZATION DEVELOPMENT

Two questions immediately spring to mind. Is there a discipline which specifically deals with culture, change and consultancy? And where can one find worthy practitioners?

The first question can more easily be answered. The terms 'culture change', 'ownership', and 'facilitation' have been in common managerial use for perhaps ten years. Their use has grown as the business world has grown more turbulent and imperatives for change have become more pressing. These terms are in danger of becoming clichés through repeated, imprecise use.

Large-scale corporate change has come of age, and consequently a market has sprung up in it. In the 1980s, in Britain, the management consultancy market grew by 30 per cent year on year, most years. There were no barriers to entry and anybody could babble that culture was 'the way we do things here' and make extravagant promises to deliver change. Alas, promises are promises and delivery is rare. Many companies, however, boasted of culture change when they had achieved nothing of the sort. This was a pity. Much money and effort was wasted and the field acquired a reputation for being peopled by hucksters.

The only discipline which specifically deals with the subject of organizational change is organization development, OD for short. It began in America after the end of World War II, when certain people became concerned with the existence of huge, inflexible 'dinosaur' organizations.

This is not the place to discuss OD in detail. Suffice it to say that there is nearly fifty years of research, writing and consultancy about change which is specific to the OD discipline and no other. OD is not training, management development or occupational psychology. It uses concepts drawn from psychology and sociology; most bona fide OD consultants will have extensive backgrounds in both subjects. However, OD is its own discipline, no other. It has its own focus – successful organizational change.

OD consultants, whether internal or external, occupy marginal roles in organizations. However extensive their involvement, externals especially, they are present on a temporary basis. The good ones tend to be highly individualistic, self-determined and even a little feisty – exactly the sort of people who, ironically, are less interested in creating organizations of their own. It is because OD practitioners have been so individualistic that the movement, the discipline, has suffered. One consequence is that today, fifty years on, it is largely unknown. Another consequence is that other disciplines have stolen OD concepts and peddled them as their own, without sufficiently understanding the concepts. Method can be like fast food: easy, accessible, convenient. Methodology requires culinary skills of a high order.

So, if you want people who really understand what change is about, search in the OD field. To find a good practitioner, however, is more difficult. Ultimately, it must be the person whose competence is most impressive. Good luck!

AN HISTORICAL APPROACH TO CHANGE

In Part I, I made the point that it can take many years for organizations to develop their distinctive cultures. Culture arises as a historical process. This seemingly obvious statement is seldom appreciated by so-called agents of change. Again and again, I have found that the way to understand organizations has been to delve into the past.

This is a strange business. Often, one feels like a strange sort of industrial archaeologist, digging away for scraps of knowledge which will provide vital clues. Long-departed managers live on as ghostly influences. Incidents have happened which, seemingly, can never be forgotten.

To understand these ghosts, one must first identify them. Autocratic pioneers, in particular, can exert substantial influence years after they have retired to the seaside. Such ghosts often have to be exorcized; their styles are the styles of yesteryear, not today.

To help people to change, to create a new future, you must first understand their present. To understand their present, you must understand their past. This can only be achieved by considering the historical influences which have been at work.

The act of understanding an organization's past and present is a highly creative one. You need a knack for seeking out the right people, making the right approaches and asking the right questions. Who these people are depends on the situation but in every organization the following four types will be found. These types were identified long ago by Jack Douglas, a student of organizational change. In nearly every organization, all four types will yield invaluable research.

THE HISTORIAN

This person has been with the organization for a long time. They can tell you what happened years ago. Their memory probably extends further than the memories of the present senior management team. They know what has transpired. Their memories may have been gilded by the passage of time but they can provide you with information which no one else can.

THE PHILOSOPHER

This person has thought long and hard about the purpose of the organization. Not content with merely observing events, they have reflected upon the meaning of such events. Their insights are invaluable. Cross-referencing their insights with the historian's knowledge can yield productive results.

THE SOCIAL GADFLY

This is the person who knows anybody and everybody, who is seemingly on good terms with all parties. He or she flits between departments, across visible and invisible lines of power and prestige, up and down the hierarchy with breathtaking ease. Often their job will legitimize this role. They will be a linker, a liaison person, a personnel manager. They can effortlessly diagnose the informal organization because they know it like the back of their hands. The cartels, the power groups, the secret societies, they know them all. Social gadflies are possessed of a high level of political adroitness. Whatever their job, in reality they function as wheeler-dealers. Historians tell you about the past; philosophers interpret the purpose; social gadflies tell you about the present – in excruciatingly vivid detail.

THE REBEL

The rebel will tell you what no one else will. The rebel gives you the downside. While the corporate mission preaches openness and trust, the rebel will tell you how little openness and trust there is in practice. The company report loftily states that 'people are our greatest asset'. The rebel will tell you, chapter and verse, of incidents which clearly demonstrate how 'they couldn't give a damn about people'.

Rebels get behind the rhetoric of organizations. Rebels will make you aware of the hypocrisies, the contradictions, the paradoxes about which you emphatically need to know. You need to understand what organizational life is really like; rebels will tell you.

Rebels are often talented people who have been rejected by an organization which could not understand them and felt threatened by their talent. Very often they are embittered. As with historians, one must scrape away at the gilded lily for the truth. Sometimes they occupy surprisingly senior positions; invariably they have been pushed sideways, relegated to marginal roles. Rebels are particularly worth listening to on the subject of change.

Here we have four different types which are present in nearly every organization. Of course, more than one type can be present in the same person. The usual overlap tends to be between historian/philosopher – the other types tend to be separate. They all belong to the informal organization, which you need to understand, better than anyone else, if change is to work.

THE ENERGY FOR CHANGE

Whatever the rhetoric, the reality is that in any organization some people will be excited about change and some people will dread it. Although it may not be politic for people to reveal their true feelings, there will be a continuum of people from those who actively want change to those who equally actively don't want it. One needs to know where people feature on this continuum.

Let's briefly consider the four categories in turn.

ACTIVELY FOR CHANGE

These people are dissatisfied with the status quo, perceive the need for change and are willing to make considerable effort to attain such change. They do not merely agree; they commit.

PASSIVELY FOR CHANGE

These people may equally accept the rationale for change. However, they are much less willing to pursue it. They agree, rather than commit.

PASSIVELY AGAINST CHANGE

These people do not want change to happen. They may agree to change but their agreement is in truth rejection. They cannot be relied on.

ACTIVELY AGAINST CHANGE

These people know where they stand. They are against change and they are prepared to fight it all the way, if necessary.

Note that all four categories belong to the informal organization. A board of directors, supposedly committed to change, will often contain people who are secretly passively against change. Quite often, it will contain at least one person who is actively against change. The most important categories are those who are actively for and those who are actively against change, but all four categories are important for different reasons.

In an organization-wide change programme, everyone will be directly or indirectly affected. Nevertheless, there will be certain players who will be fundamental to the success of the programme. They will be fundamental because they occupy key positions in either the formal or informal organizations. They have leadership roles in crucial domains.

These people must become actively for change if the programme is to have any chance of success. Because they are, or tend to be, leaders anyway, they will probably already be either actively for or actively against change.

Surprisingly, many people who are initially actively against change become actively for change. This is because, sometimes, the actively againsts are the rebels whom I mentioned in the last section. They will say, for example, 'Sure, the board are making all these lofty statements and bringing in consultants. But they're just a bunch of milksops. They've had these so-called initiatives before. They've had consultants in before. Nothing changed. Why should this be any different?'

This is grist to the mill of someone who is serious about change because the question must be answered fairly and squarely. Other initiatives have failed. Why should this one be any different? Intellectually, people need to be pinned to the wall. The change programme was probably conceived as yet another evasion of reality – more dysfunctional behaviour. People need to be sharply disabused of this notion.

There is no question of pandering to rebels. But treating them as competent beings – as they invariably are – will often bear curious results. If their scathing honesty produces questions which should be asked and answered, and these questions *are* asked and answered, then, very often, they will be turned round. More precisely, they will turn themselves round.

Other rebels are people with qualities, such as creativity, which are neither understood nor appreciated by the organization. Often these qualities are the very ones needed for engendering change. I have known rebels who waited all their working lives for the opportunity to show what they were capable of. When they realized that the opportunity had finally arrived (and it wasn't another management fad), they were revitalized. My goodness, how they shone.

Other people who often are against change are people who are so frustrated that their energies are almost completely negative. This is invariably because change is long overdue. They are perhaps suffering in a pioneer organization which has failed to make the transition to a systems organization. Their working lives are made a misery because of poor operational planning and control – control which is, ironically, invariably resisted for cultural reasons. They are in a complete no-win situation. Their achievements seem pathetic; they regard themselves as worthless failures. They are against change because they are so frustrated and negative that they are against anything and everything. Their very high level of existing frustration makes them frightened of considering any solution to their problems – in case their hopes are raised and then dashed. This is particularly poignant if such hopes have been raised and dashed before.

In situations like this, seemingly paradoxically, one has to work with their negative energy, because that is the dominant force. Although these people are anti-change, they are also anti the status quo. If they really do believe that change is possible and they see results, then their negative energy will be converted to positive energy. Why shouldn't it be? They will be getting what they wanted. They will no longer be losers; they will become winners.

Enabling such people to turn themselves round is no easy task. It requires powers of moral leadership which few possess. It is the sort of quality which is needed for real, worthwhile, sustainable change in organizations, the sort of quality of which the hatchet man and the management faddist will never even conceive.

It is because most change initiatives are overdue that this need to work with negative energy to create positive energy is often encountered. It is, perhaps, the organizational change specialist's particular form of the alchemist's dream by which base metals are converted to gold.

Can all those who are actively against change be enabled to turn themselves around? Typically, there will be people who for reasons of status, prestige, power, personality or belief will remain against change. It is essential that such people are identified and relevant issues confronted. Difference must be managed. Either there are amendments to make or there are selfish motives at work. Whichever, the issues must be confronted and resolved – or the change process is seriously at risk. Thus the absolute importance of assertiveness, as mentioned earlier. People will want to shirk such confrontation and resolution, they will want to bypass it. But they must not. This requires real skill and real courage. People's right to dissent must be regarded as legitimate, but it must be regarded as equally legitimate that a solution needs to be negotiated. Not to resolve such dissent is unacceptable.

Culture change is people change. Culture change cannot reasonably be made to happen any more than a flower can be made to grow. Good gardeners do not try to make flowers grow; they enable them to grow. So it is with people change. You are working above all with those who are actively for change while remaining highly cognizant of everyone else. From the remains of the old culture, you are growing a new culture. From positive and from negative energy, you are working to create positive energy.

Figure 19 illustrates the curve of commitment. Superficially, this resembles the classic marketing curve of response to new products. However, the biggest difference is in the existence of people vehemently actively against – and the divided nature of such people. They can be the old guard, who composed the status quo of yesteryear, or they can be the rebels who were once rigorously suppressed. It can be a strange phenomenon in a change project to see the establishment disband and the rebels come to power. Perhaps we shouldn't be too surprised; Machiavelli, who had his own views on change, would not have been.

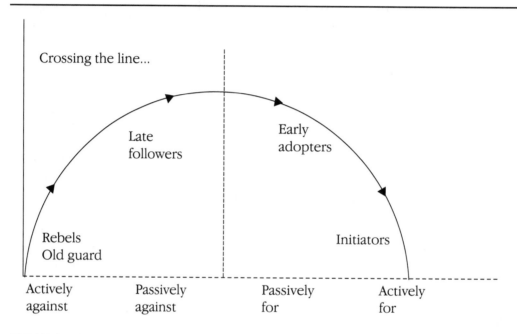

FIGURE 19   THE CURVE OF COMMITMENT

Through working with negative and positive energy to create positive energy, one is, of course, building up energy to a **critical mass**. At this point, commitment for change dwarfs commitment against change. People who were passively for change become actively for change. The people who were passively against change become passively for change.

If one imagines a line drawn down the middle of Figure 19, then the aim of a change project is to enable people to come across that line. When this happens, it's easier to go on than to turn back. Again, I stress that getting people across that line is no easy task. Results obviously help, for results are the best possible advertisement for a change process. I can think of at least one important project (in which I did not partic-ipate) where the initial results – for entirely noble motives – were massaged. (Subsequent results were bona fide.) In all honesty, I have to say that I would strenu-ously oppose this tactic, even though it did raise morale considerably. The risk of being caught out and thus being discredited is too high. Also it seems to me to be rather demeaning. Besides, nothing corrupts a change process faster than 'insider dealing', regardless of whether the motives are worthwhile. Change works on mutual trust; this needs to be sacred.

When critical mass is achieved, the initiators of change can breathe a sigh of relief. The worst is over.

THE POLITICAL NATURE OF CHANGE

Politics at work is a social phenomonen which everyone knows about yet which most people fight shy of confronting. Certainly it is little mentioned in management text-books; the prevailing assumption is that everyone is diligently digging for victory for the greater glory of the organization. The chance would be a fine thing!

This is a **unitary** notion – we're all one, we're willing parts of a collective whole. The alternative is **pluralism**, which postulates that there are many different power groups, with their own agendas. Anyone who has read the section on the social reality of organizations (p. 24), will not be surprised that I find the pluralist viewpoint a more intellectually honest depiction of what we all know goes on.

Nevertheless, not only do management textbooks ignore the political nature of pluralism but so also do most approaches to change management. TQM, for instance, seems to credit us with a unitary collectivism which may or may not exist in Japan but which rarely exists here. To ignore organizational politics when managing change is to fail. What then is the alternative? Should one be political?

The short answer is no. You should not be political. If you do become political, then professional integrity is sacrificed. You are just another silver-tongued hustler parad-ing your wares while seeking to manipulate. This is the road to disaster.

Politics does not add value. It is an overhead which, in many organizations, should be sharply reduced. There is a school of thought which postulates that organizations are backcloths against which the ruthless act. The ruthless are never satisfied until they have made a deal too many. The rest of us pay for such indulgence.

To facilitate change, you need to be highly politically aware and highly politically adept – while remaining apolitical. How can this be? You are not using your skills on your own behalf, or even on behalf of any power group. Rather, they are genuinely being used on behalf of an agreed consensus.

In many organizations, those who are regarded as political are thereby credited with a high degree of political prowess. This is rarely the case. Often they are local heroes who would be destroyed if they moved out of their familiar environment. Being political does not necessarily equate with political prowess. Possession of political prowess does not necesarily equate with being political.

So to ignore politics is futile. Politics, like everything else, must be managed. To be political is equally futile. In practice, I admit, it is rare to find people who do possess a high degree of political prowess but steadfastly do not use it for their own ends. Such people do exist, however. In your search for a process consultant, I would recommend that this seemingly contradictory pair of factors constitutes a key assessment criterion. As a colleague of mine once remarked, 'Part of what you're selling is that you can't be bought.'

Therefore politics must be managed and it must be managed well. Much dysfunctional political behaviour in organizations results from frustration, often frustration from symptoms whose core problems change will resolve. In many organizations, everyone – victims and oppressors alike – shares a common victimhood due to conditions which, it seems, no one can ameliorate. The downtrodden foreman can be a victim; so too can the supposedly omnipotent chief executive. The shop floor worker can be aching with frustration; so can the managing director. Ordinarily, they might never realize this, but those who manage change must realize it and enable them to realize it also. Losers must be transformed into winners. All of us want to be winners. In any case, in the modern business world, there is no place for losers.

So you are aiming to achieve positive outcomes for many different power groups. To do so, you will have to create a space for assertive behaviour where weapons can be put aside and issues truly resolved. This space must be enlarged so that, finally, it encompasses the whole organization. Again, you are looking for critical mass.

The path to this critical mass is fraught. There will invariably have been many ill-conceived, poorly skilled and executed attempts which have failed. Understandably, people will be cynical. To deliver organizational change is always to succeed where others have failed.

Change which creates winners and losers will also fail; the losers will sabotage it. Whatever the difficulties, however fearsome the issues, people must be helped through them to personally acceptable outcomes. Process consultancy, facilitation ... of course anyone can do it!

Change is by its very nature political. It is part of the informal organization, the social reality. It must be managed and managed well.

THE NEGOTIATIVE PARADIGM

Underlying the reasoning of the previous section is the notion that in organizational life everything is negotiable. A little thought reveals that this makes sense. If management is about solving problems, resolving issues, then the sort of collaborative assertive behaviour described in the section on conflict (see p. 129) is the way forward. This implicitly recognizes the existence of pluralism; it regards conflict as inevitable and legitimate. It also regards resolution of such conflict as utterly necessary. On this basis, the path of progress is issue by issue.

The old, simple notion of conflict between workers and management is absurdly simplistic today. Today there are few free lunches for anyone. Only direct labour is wealth-producing; the rest of us are overheads who must prove ourselves by indirectly aiding the wealth (or, in a non-profit-making organization, the social added value) process. All of us will have our own agendas; we must work through these agendas to issue resolution, or we will all fail together.

The negotiative paradigm sounds like a bland middle-class term. It isn't. It simply recognizes that different people have different viewpoints. Such differences need resolving. In the past, many companies could afford passive workforces who came to work, sweated their labour and were told to shut up. In today's climate of relentless, continuous improvement, the lathe operator as well as the company director must be motivated and involved. This being the case, he or she must be a valued partner. The negotiative paradigm is the only responsible approach.

THE MANAGEMENT OF DIFFERENCE

Again, this approach recognizes that we are different, with different histories, personalities, agendas. Unitary approaches to organizational change management will fail because they do not take account of reality. Ironically, through managing difference, one will create a far more focused organization. Differences between individuals, in groups and between groups must all be managed. It's difficult but it can be done. It needs to be done.

THE POWER OF INFORMATION

The role of information was considered in Part I. To improve performance in organizations, to create new behaviour and new results, one needs MCS – management control systems. Few organizations have them; all organizations need them. They can be imposed to control people, in which case, as far as change is concerned, they are counterproductive. Alternatively they can be developed by the people themselves, primarily for their own use. Management control systems engender discipline. The best discipline and the only one ultimately worth having is self-discipline.

Management control systems need to go from the bottom to the top of management hierarchies, however flat, and back down again. They encourage top-down and bottom-up change. They help define role. They do not of themselves progress change but their *use* can progress change. Similarly, they should never be passively followed; they should always be created hand in hand with people development. By helping people to create and use management control systems, the act of creation can itself be developmental.

Information is value free; information is apolitical. Our use of information is everything. Change initiatives which do not have an information infrastructure will miss their focus. We all need the necessary information in order to improve our performance. Culture change is ultimately about sustained improved performance. The right information for the right people at the right time is mandatory.

DEVELOPMENTAL CHANGE AND PROJECT MANAGEMENT

Earlier I noted that you cannot reasonably *make* people culturally change. You can only *help* them culturally to change. Change is organic, creative. The great danger here is that change initiatives diverge, become open-ended. This is professionally unacceptable – because it means that the focus on particular behaviour and results is lost. It is also commercially unacceptable for two reasons. There is no end date to aim at and it presupposes a blank cheque for financing the entire process.

Change needs to be organic. Often one is working with energy in the informal organization. Change also needs to occur under conditions of strict project management, otherwise it will not succeed.

These two approaches may seem to contradict each other. One is organic, and the other is mechanistic. On the face of it, they do contradict each other. But that's tough. Both are necessary.

I have spoken to managers who have proudly told me that they have spent years facilitating culture change – and they are still doing so. When will they finish? And how would they know if they had finished? What is their methodology, which are their methods, where is their information, where, above all, are the enhanced results? Of course, on questioning, none of these appear. So what have these managers been doing? Probably talking a good fight and feeling proud of it!

The fact is that change needs superlative project management skills. It does not need projects which are ill-conceived – as are the projects in Part II. It does not need projects which go off the rails, as do the projects in Part III. It does not need projects which suffer from slippage.

Change means a different reality. It is a game of reality; it is not a game of fantasy, of make-believe. Change programmes should come in on time and to cost. Show me a good change agent and I'll show you an excellent people developer and a superb project manager. Again they're rare; again they exist. To manage the subtle, the creative, the nebulous, the unknown – by superlative process consultancy – yet within the context of zero slippage project management, this truly is the realm of the sorcerer.

SHORTENING THE LEAD TIME

In Part I the point was made that for many organizations the lead time of culture change was vital for their survival. More precisely, shortening the lead time is vital. On a practical level, this book is aimed at helping people to shorten the lead time. There are many seductive and misleading pathways, many blind alleys. And there is much to be done.

It is erroneously assumed that change is commonplace, and because of this many managers' concepts of change are naive, limiting and ultimately self-defeating. Change is often construed as something which is poured into people as water is poured into a jar. On this basis, statements will be made such as, 'Our people can't handle any more change at present. We've got a three-year IT development programme and we're setting up modules for managerial training. So we're working on transforming our culture. Yes, of course, we accept that operational improvement is there to be gained. But we can't risk overloading our people.'

Overloading is a genuine fear. When people are overloaded, useful learning ceases. But this approach assumes that people are only learning about change in terms of the content of this change and the content of that change.

The road to real progress does not lie in passively learning about the content of specific changes. It lies in learning about the process of change itself. The process of change is far more important than the content. Get the process wrong and the content may well be brilliant but it will also be useless.

So, if you learn about the process of change and utilize this learning in terms of specific contents, progress will not be linear; it will be exponential. Think what this could mean for your survival; think what it could do to your competition.

Learning about change will involve learning to learn. When I was a student, I could read (and understand?) perhaps a chapter of a textbook in one study session. Now I routinely read and understand whole books at a sitting. More importantly, before, the knowledge was passive; now it is dynamic. I'm cross-referencing it to everything else I know which is remotely relevant. And most importantly of all, I'm transforming the knowledge into practical use.

If I can improve my ability to learn by a multiple of ten (probably much more), then so can you – and so can your people. For all of us, the real classroom is the real world. Don't give your people boring instruction. Bring out the knowledge, the maturity, the need, the desire. And then stand well back!

Shortening the lead time of change – any change – will probably determine whether you're around in a few years' time. Enough said.

PEOPLE POWER

We've heard it before and we'll hear it again. 'People are this company's greatest asset!' Show me the evidence? Oh, I'm sorry.... There isn't any.

I am writing during the most long-lived recession of this century. In the UK some three million people are out of work; many of them have been thrown on to the proverbial scrap heap. Do they still regard themselves as their company's greatest assets? Pause for hollow laughter....

We need less empty rhetoric, more good practice. There are no jobs for life for any of us. The passive process worker who just came in, did his work and knew his place is an industrial dinosaur. So is the company director who shuffled papers, played games in boardrooms and lived the good life. Somebody always paid for this; usually it was the customer. Now nobody will. It's over.

There is no more room for tedium, for treating people like monkeys and paying them peanuts, for sloppy management. Now it really is do or die.

People *are* a company's greatest asset; they've got to be. A machine is finite; people aren't. People are capable of infinite development, of massive gains in productivity, in quality. In our global village, the chances are that your competitors have access to the same information, the same technology. Your competitive edge is people.

At the turn of the century, F.W. Taylor, the father of work study and one of the most misunderstood men in the history of management, said that more important than his work was what he called 'a mental revolution'. That mental revolution has come of age. It is called culture change.

THE CULTURE ICEBERG

Figure 20 illustrates the perennial situation. The new boys – and girls – draw near to the iceberg. They are not fools; they know that the future is fraught with peril. They can see behaviour and results; they are aware of expectation. They can even make a good guess at attitude.

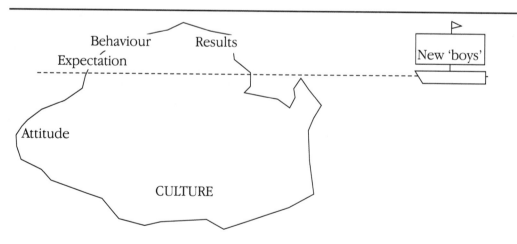

FIGURE 20   THE CULTURE ICEBERG

Meanwhile, beneath the surface of awareness, lies culture – vast, amorphous, possessed of illimitable power. What will happen to the newcomers? What will happen to the iceberg? Who can tell?

TOWARDS THE FUTURE

An ancient Chinese curse runs, 'May you live in interesting times.' We do live in interesting times – information explosion and market contraction in terms of key players; global consumerism and global recession; social and political unrest; the harsh imperative of a primordial drive which states that we must have more than our parents and that our children must have more than us; mass expectations that economies, of whatever political ideology, should deliver, bitter resentment when they don't.

As we approach the end of the millenium, will life somehow quieten down? Will the business, social, political and economic environments become more or less turbulent?

I think the answer will be 'more turbulent'. You probably feel likewise. Certainly we would want long odds to bet on the answer being 'less'. More turbulence, more complexity, more change. More change in the rate of change. It's frightening.

Organizations are the crucial interface between the micro and the macro. If we fail at an organizational level then we fail at every level. This is such an appalling prospect that we dare not even contemplate it. We *must* make organizations work.

Culture and change are the dominant themes of organizations today. If we manage them successfully then our tomorrows can be immeasurably better. I hope that we do.

Empowering People at Work

Nancy Foy

This is a book written, says the author, "for the benefit of practical managers coping with real people in real organizations". Part I shows how the elements of empowerment work together: performance focus, teams, leadership and face-to-face communication. Part II explains how to manage the process of empowerment, even in a climate of "downsizing" and "delayering". It includes chapters on networking, listening, running effective team meetings, giving feedback, training and using employee surveys. Part III contains case studies of IBM and British Telecom and examines the way they have developed employee communication to help achieve corporate objectives.

The final section comprises a review of communication channels that can be used to enhance the empowerment process, an extensive set of survey questions to be selected on a "pick and mix" basis and an annotated guide to further reading.

Empowerment is probably the most important concept in the world of management today, and Nancy Foy's new book will go a long way towards helping managers to "make it happen".

Contents

1994   288 pages   0 566 07436 2

Gower

How Managers Can Develop Managers

Alan Mumford

Managers are constantly being told that they are responsible for developing other managers. This challenging book explains why and how this should be done.

Moving beyond the familiar territory of appraisal, coaching and courses, Professor Mumford examines ways of using day-to-day contact to develop managers. The emphasis is on learning from experience - from the job itself, from problems and opportunities, from bosses, mentors and colleagues.

Among the topics covered are:
- recognizing learning opportunities
- understanding the learning process
- what being helped involves
- the skills required to develop others
- the idea of reciprocity ("I help you, you help me")

Throughout the text there are exercises designed to connect the reader's own experience to the author's ideas. The result is a powerful and innovative work from one of Europe's foremost writers on management development.

Contents

1993   240 pages   0 566 07403 6

Gower

A Manual for Change

Terry Wilson

Change is now the only constant, as the cliché has it, and organizations who fail to master change are likely to find themselves undone by it.

In this unique manual, Terry Wilson provides the tools for planning and implementing a systematic organizational change programme. The first section enables the user to determine the scope and scale of the programme. Next, a change profile is completed based on twelve key factors. Finally, each of the factors is reviewed in the context of the user's own organization. Questionnaries and exercises are provided throughout and any manager working through these will have not only a clear understanding of the change process but also specific plans ready to put into action.

Derived from the author's experience of working with organizations at every level and in a wide range of industries, the manual will be invaluable to directors, managers, consultants and professional trainers battling to help their organizations survive and flourish in an increasingly turbulent environment.

Contents

Using this manual • Change programme focus: The scale of change • Change process profile: The twelve factors • Factor one Perspectives: Maintaining the overall view • Factor two The change champion: Leading the change • Factor three The nature of change: Identifying the change affecting us • Factor four Unified management vision: Importance of management agreement • Factor five Change of organizational philosophy: Modernizing the organization • Factor six Change phases: Four phases of change • Factor seven The 10/90 rule: Vision and real change • Factor eight Transitional management: Management role and style • Factor nine Teamwork: Importance of teams • Factor ten Changing behaviour: Identifying the critical factors • Factor eleven Expertise and resources: Assessing requirements • Factor twelve Dangers and pitfalls: Planning to avoid difficulties.

1994   192 pages   0 566 07460 5

Gower

The
Motivation Manual

Gisela Hagemann

Improved productivity, flexible work practices, low rates of absenteeism, commitment to quality, ever-higher standards of customer service -these are the benefits of a well-motivated workforce. In this prize-winning book the author takes modern motivational theory and shows how any manager can apply it to create shared vision, develop mutual trust and involve employees in the decision-making process.

The text is enlivened throughout by examples with which managers will identify and there is a unique final section containing twenty seven exercises designed to strengthen interpersonal skills and improve creativity.

Contents

1992   210 pages   0 566 07295 5

Gower

Problem Solving in Groups

Second Edition

Mike Robson

Modern scientific research has demonstrated that groups are likely to solve problems more effectively than individuals. As most of us knew already, two heads (or more) are better than one. In organizations it makes sense to harness the power of the group both to deal with problems already identified and to generate ideas for enhancing effectiveness by reducing costs, increasing productivity and the like.

In this revised and updated edition of his successful book, Mike Robson first introduces the concepts and methods involved. Then, after setting out the advantages of the group approach, he examines in detail each of the eight key problem solving techniques. The final part of the book explains how to present proposed solutions, how to evaluate results and how to ensure that the group process runs smoothly.

With its practical tone, its down-to-earth style and lively visuals, this is a book that will appeal strongly to managers and trainers looking for ways of improving their organization's and their department's performance.

Contents

1993   176 pages   0 566 07414 1 Hardback   0 566 07415 X Paperback

Gower